Teen Angst Mix Tape Vol.2

Copyright © 2022. All rights reserved.

4 Horsemen Publications, Inc.
1497 Main St. Suite 169
Dunedin, FL 34698
4horsemenpublications.com
info@4horsemenpublications.com

Cover by Battle Goddess Productions
Typesetting by Autumn Skye
Editor Vanessa Valiente

All rights to the work within are reserved to the author and publisher. No part of this publication may be reproduced, stored in a retrieval system, or transmitted in any form or by any means, electronic, mechanical, photocopying, recording, scanning, or otherwise, except as permitted under Section 107 or 108 of the 1976 International Copyright Act, without prior written permission except in brief quotations embodied in critical articles and reviews. Please contact either the Publisher or Author to gain permission.

Library of Congress Control Number: 2022944226

Ebook ISBN: 978-1-64450-285-3

Print ISBN: 978-1-64450-286-0

Contents

Beth W. Patterson - Runaway..... 7

Daniel Reece - Blodeuwedd 15

Anabelle Cusi - An Accident Love Story 17

Adam Lee - Witch............23

Abigail Maixner - Teen Anguish. 27

Katherine M. - When you know. 35

Patricia P. - 10:26om........... 37

Megan F. - Heartstrings? 39

Anjoline D. - Diary.............. 41

Lex M. - Emails to Myself 63

Kaley C. - Untitled............. 65

Regan D. - Journal Entry 64 .. 69

Soroya K. - Untitled...........73

Laura G. - I Know 77

Josephine E. - Letter to Rendezvous........... 81

K S. - Times Lost 87

Anna Z. - I love Lara........... 89

Rocio C. - How does it feel to be known 93

Sophia R. - Some People 97

Jayden M. - Jamie........... 101

Sara T. - Lonely 105

Aushima V. - Am I So Worthless.......... 107

Tina H. - Untitled 111

Gabrielle M.- Untitled 117

Ozzy P. - 3 Years............. 119

Regan Z. - The Last Game..... 123

Morgan H. - Personal Essay ...127

Sakshi S. - And I Smile 131

Trinity M. - 1-22-22........ 135

- Hannah S. - Always the Man . 143
- Summer O. - Random First Line 145
- Piper K. - Untitled 151
- Lucas T. C. - Untitled 155
- Paige D. - I believe in Nothing 159
- Marie-Belle M. - Poems 1,2 &3 165
- Elliott Cochran - Autobiography 169
- Kate Feagan - Creative Writing Short 173
- Riya Gupta - Peace 179

INTRODUCTION:

Hello Reader,

Welcome to our second Teen Angst mixtape aka Vol 2.

We hope you enjoy the stories, poems, and diary entries from this year. You should know that we do not change any content that is submitted. It is as it was given to us.

There are so many stories, thoughts, and dreams presented here. We are fortunate to have submissions from people that are well out of their teens and those still in the middle of life, as a teenager, at this moment.

As someone who ended their teenage years in the early nineties, I want to offer a few words. First, being a teenager can be **difficult**. This difficulty is compounded by the media, government, friends, and parents who at times do not remember what it is like to be a teenanger because the world has changed since they were that age.

However, I will say this: You can make it better. You have a choice.

There are so many adventures from your teenage years forward. You get to decide what you want to be when you grow up over and over again. There are so many adventures to be had, so long as you are willing to take the actions to have them. Life will be what you make of it.

Most importantly, you are **NOT ALONE**. I can promise you there is someone out there who will listen when you need it, offer you advice, and cheer as you make your successes. You simply have to ask.

So with that, I present our Angst for 2022!

LOVE AND HUGS,

Erika Lance
CEO 4 Horsemen Publications
Author
Actor
Cosplayer
& Nerd (Before it was Cool)

xoxo

RUNAWAY

Date: Fall, 1990

The old me

Who you were then: I had just started my senior year in high school in the Cajun town of Lafayette, Louisiana. My impending adulthood--specifically others' expectations of such--was a *parasite* in my mind. The previous year I had decided that I didn't want to have children, and that I just wanted to travel as far and wide as possible playing music. I had already discussed the possibility of **MARRIAGE** with a boy I was crazy about. He was an accomplished musician, but he didn't want to leave Louisiana and he definitely had fatherhood in mind.

I wanted independence, and I loved playing my bass guitar. (I also didn't know at the time that the use of the word "*gypsy*" to apply to someone with insatiable wanderlust would someday no longer be acceptable. My apologies to my readers of Romani descent, as well as the travelers I later met in Ireland and Scotland.)

I was so brainwashed by the belief that settling down and procreating was practically mandatory, I secretly grappled with this issue quite a bit, such as in this poem.

The NEW me!

Who you are now: I went on to be a music major at Loyola University in New Orleans. Academic life was never my thing either, but I didn't have any prospects of going straight from high school to a working band situation. I did, however, get an oboe scholarship, which partially put a dorm roof over my head.

It wasn't long before I was playing five nights a week in the FRENCH QUARTER on bass and Irish bouzouki, drinking insane amounts of coffee to simultaneously meet school requirements. Eventually I played in various groups (some of which toured). I later pursued a solo career, which was more taxing but allowed me a more personal journey.

At the time of writing, I have released eight solo albums, appeared on over two hundred recordings, played in nineteen countries across five countries...and I have no children. I'm forever outraged at people's negative treatment of childless women. I hope that I will live to see a day when adolescent girls don't have to vent on paper in secret, and that they know from an early age that their bodies are no one else's business.

And I'm married to a fine musician who never wanted to be a parent either. People used to give him **grief** about that too!

Beth Wagoner
Fall, 1990

Runaway

From restless dreams I tear myself awake
To find myself in the confines of security
Warm in the clutches of fidelity
Fat from my luxury

The tops of the trees in the distance look
 like a line of elephants
Year after year I have watched them
They have never moved an inch

The egret glides to greet them
Unbound by morals or broken dreams
Yet returning to the same nest every year

I am aware of the tiny stirrings
Wondering souls in miniature
I see my eyes in their drowsy faces
As I see to it that they are dressed and
 fed
And well on their way to school

The house is quiet now
But the old familiar silent call pulls
 at my heart
And I head toward the dark, dusty
 service

Waggoner 9; 7

Blow away the cobwebs and hail
  my old friend
Whose low voice pulses like a heartbeat
As my hands, weakened by years of
  disuse
Glide across the smooth, polished wood,
Steel strings as taut as my nerves
My surroundings dissolve around me
In my most sinful affair

And ~~I became~~ the past
Who I once was
Hopeful, fearful, courageous, heroic
Free

When my flight is over, the present
  reality is a shock
The dark room a shadow of my fate
I see a stranger's face in the mirror
Creased and hardened from overwhelming
  bonds
Coarsened from domestic life
Hair gone dark, flesh gone white
From never seeing the light

Waggoner 3

Too often have felt this, now
If the best things in life come
   to those who wait
Then I might have spread my wings
But hastily, in my youth, I burned the
   bridge ahead of me without a
   second thought
And, once again, I can wait no
   longer
A gypsy must roam

I once broke family traditions
   with my reckless ways
I discarded the art of conformity
   with a sneer
I now break the cycle that I
   once thought inevitable as death —
Glorious days of youth slowly
   going cold
In teaching those following to
   do the same
I will finish my long-forgotten
   quest
And find a place where I can
   never die

Wagoner No. 4

The rising sun casts a golden veil
　through the window
Onto my bass case
I grab the handle, feeling the
　familiar weight pull with annoyance
at my ^weakened arms:
Where the hell have you been?

A cup of coffee. A cold piece of chicken.
　Half a banana and some pie...
Money from my last paycheck. My
　old switchblade. Spare strings...
Rip up an old letter. Throw out
　the tattered, bloodstained sheet...
Hurry, hurry, my life gets shorter by
　the second...
Blankets. My amp. Phone numbers.
　Soap. Toothbrush...

In the morning light my old van
　gleams
The sun's rays caress my cold flesh
I laugh out loud at the tears that
　threaten to burst forth

12 TEEN ANGST

Waggoner J.S.
AA

My keys feel strangely heavy in my hand
Barely used, they rattle musically
What will I use for my parting shot?
I love them all so, but my compulsions drive me onward
Where I cannot let them follow.

DON'T SEARCH FOR ME.
I WON'T BE THERE.
I LOVE YOU ALL.

They always knew.
I spring to the driver's seat,
slide my bass in the passenger's side
Ignition...
The engine roars triumphantly —
Blast off!

I have no past now
Just a higher reverence for my stiffened wings.

Mix Tape Vol. 2 Runaway 13

BLODEUWEDD

Date: 1995

The old me

Who you were then: I was an 18 year old college freshman, just married and my wardrobe was 90% **black**.

The NEW me!

Who you are now: Still married to the same girl 26 years later. Wardrobe is still mostly **black** but a lot more khaki.

Tulips brushed across her face
As I lay her down in this garden place
The forest is quiet, dark and deep
A tearful willow starts to weep

Protective golems sit in silence
Tried to warn you and keep you from *violets*
Roses, roses from which my hand BLED
As you sew in your flower bed

See the busy **bee** unsettle
Flirting each petal to petal
Pollinating as its nature is
Claiming all the *flowers* his

Feel the heat and cold of lust
These *marigolds* have turned to dust
Blue bells ring, and so I heard
Chrysanthemums the word.

An Accident Love Story

Date: 2002

The old me

Who you were then: That time, me and my family was living in a **FAR AWAY ISLAND**. Our school is very far from our house. We need to walk almost 2 hours to reach our school, back and forth everyday. This poem describes my four years in high school having this special person. He was my first *love*. My everyday life in school is always special because of him. But I *BROKE* up with him months before our graduation because I will be studying in the city very far from the island.

The NEW me!

Who you are now: I have my own family now having 2 kids. My husband is working in Saudi Arabia and I am managing our apartment and printing business.

As I looked back in our past,
On how we started and last,
It all began in an accident,
An accidentally united by the love it sent.

The four years of my high school is such a ladder,
Not just for my academics to be better
It is also a witness for our story to grow
From friends, to infatuation until we love each other so.

(1st year)
We were just good friends that time,
And it was our last day for our clearance to be sign,
Everyone was busy completing the requirements,
And I don't know the accident that I will meet.

As I gave my papers to the teacher
On a glass window through the small opening,
My hand was scratch on the glass
And soon bleed so much.

Don't even know that time that soon we both sooths,
I hurriedly run to our classroom to seek for a piece of cloth,
To stop the bleeding, but then you I find,
But that moment, you're just a friend in my sight,

You offered me your handkerchief,
Instead of a piece of rug that I seek,
I refused to used it and replied just a smile,
Then left you with nothing special.

(2nd year)
I already forgot what happened last school year,
But don't know why in my life you suddenly enter,
That every time we cross our path, you smile at me,
And says "Now I saw my crush, I'm already happy."

Since you always do this
I also admire you because in playing volleyball, you're the best,
That once you're in the court, my seat was moved
My feelings for you were also developed.

(3rd year)

You send me a letter saying that I'm special to you,
I don't know what to do, but in my heart, you too,
Since then, our actions are not the same,
These are the reflections of how we feel.

But sometimes, love brings not so good effect,
Whenever you're around, I'm so conscious about myself
I don't even participate in our recitation
Then came to the point that my grades became low.

But before the end of the school year,
I made my grades higher again,
With that I learn, I cannot love and study at the same time,
But this time, I don't want to say goodbye.

(4th year)

I'm so excited for this year,
Hoping this will be a continuation of the love story we share,
But love sometime, is very playful,
I don't expect that this will be a nightmare, oh no!

You said, you courted a girl but that was nothing,
That I should forget all the memories we share,
Its very painful for me, my tears want to fall,
But I don't want you to see me crying, so I control.

That whole day seems such a terror,
Then at night, I cried and cried more,
My heart was very painful, it wants to explode,
Blaming myself why my love for you brings wounds.

The next day brings a new side of me,
I wrote a letter, "Its ok, goodbye", I say
A stronger self that can carry on
I can forget you very soon.

But this heartache seems such a play,
That we must hate each other, I supposed to be
Its such an irony, that we become more close,
Everyday, we have a letter for us both.

Until one day, you walk with me to our home,
And as we walked along, you keep on asking me,
You told me that you still love me so
That you want to court me again, I don't know what to say.

I was confused what to answer,
If yes, you will court me again, how about my grades I care,
If No, I am afraid to lose you again,
So, what will I say?

After walking afar, you stop awhile,
You asked again a question with a smile,
This time a new one, I thought you just rephrase it,
Can we be together? You said.

A whisper "Yes" accidentally came out from my mouth,
For me it means permission to court me again, but as
a girlfriend, it's not!
I don't know why you're very happy that time,
That for me, it's a challenge to come.

After one month, you send me a letter,
Greeting me, Happy 1st Monthsarry" for being together.
I was shocked and don't know what to do.
You consider my Yes as being your girlfriend and
now what can I do?

I just follow what you consider is the meaning
For in reality, I love you still
It will be the beginning of a sweet realization
Of how accident start it and the same make the connection.

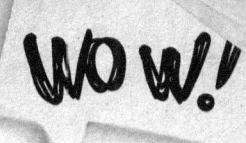

Five months has passed and now a month before graduation,
I made a decision,
To break up with you even without any big reason,
For one thing, that we'll be apart after that occasion,
At least we end up as friends again and with a good closure.

I don't want to do this but fate asked for it.
I will study afar; my time and attention for you will be different,
It's for your own good; I have to let you go.
Someone will love you more that I can do.

Not all love stories end up happily ever after,
I have to say goodbye and let you go for the better,
Even it's the hardest thing to do
For me, it means happiness and freedom for you,
that's how I love you.

I hope someday, you'll find a way to realize
Why I have to do this
That sometimes letting go is another way to say
How much I love you every day.

Although it all happened accidentally,
But our love for each other is as wonderful as it can be
For I know God has a reason why we came to each other lives,
To show how great love is and how kind it is just to
make things alright.;

WITCH

Date: 2005

The old me

Who you were then: During this time in my life, I was a sophomore in highschool, and I was being **BULLIED**. It was one girl in particular who really chipped away at me starting my freshman year. No one ever noticed or did anything, so this was kind of a dark moment in my life. Although I remember what little Adam was going through at the time and more importantly the thoughts and feelings he was having, it's still no excuse for this poem. It's so embarasing, I don't It's why I wrote it. It also doesn't help that I, like many others during the 2000s, was going through my emo phase. Wearing eyeliner daily and listening to nothing but **My Chemical Romance** instead of *Britney Spears*.

The NEW me!

Who you are now: Today, I am 32 yeas old and I hold a steady job which I love a lot. I work as practicing DOCTOR, and I've been able to overcome so many mountains with the help of my beautiful wife. We've been married for 10 years now! Time really flies by, even you're no to HAVING FUN. It was quite the experience to go back in time and see what my life was like before. And this wasn't my only poem, for some reason I thought I could write poetry and songs.

I'M NOT OKAY
NO
I'M NOT
I'M NOT OKAY

I KNOW IT'S WRONG
I KNOW IT'S BAD
AND I KNOW IT'S EVIL
BUT I HAVE SO MUCH HATE IN MY HEART

SO MUCH HATE FOR THAT WITCH
FOR THAT WITCH WHO TORMENTS ME FOR SIMPLY BREATHING
FOR THAT WITCH WHO'S TAKEN ME DOWN INTO THE DEPTHS OF DARKNESS
FOR THAT WITCH WHO NO ONE STANDS UP TO

EVERY FLAW, EVERY MISTAKE
SHE IS THERE
EVERY PIMPLE ON MY FACE
SHE POINTS IT OUT

I QUIT BAND BECAUSE IT'S NERDY
I STOPPED EATING BECAUSE I LOOK FAT
I STOPPED TALKING BECAUSE I STUTTER
I STARTED WEARING LONG SLEEVES BECAUSE I'M NOT MUSCULAR ENOUGH

ALL BECAUSE OF HER
BECAUSE OF HER AGONY AND DESPAIR THAT SHE RADIATES
BECAUSE OF HER CRUEL WAYS
THAT MAKE A BOY HATE HIMSELF SO MUCH HE DOESN'T KNOW WHAT TO DO

HE KNOWS WHAT HE WANTS TO DO
HE WANTS TO FOLLOW THROUGH
FOLLOW THROUGH THE INSTRUCTIONS SHE'S WRITTEN ON MY NOTEBOOK
THOUSANDS OF TIMES IN PERMANENT INK

KYS
KYS
KYS
KYS

BUT WHAT DOES IT MATTER
I'M THE MAN HERE AFTER ALL
I SHOULD BE ABLE TO HANDLE A FEW MEAN WORDS
ESPECIALLY FROM A GIRL

BECAUSE GIRLS ARE THE BODY CONSCIOUS ONES
BECAUSE GIRLS GET BULLIED
BECAUSE GIRLS HAVE IT WORSE
BECAUSE GIRLS DON'T DESERVE IT

IT'S OKAY
I'M OKAY
I'M FINE
IF I KEEP SAYING IT, IT HAS TO COME TRUE

I'M NOT FINEI'M NOT FINEI'M NOT FINE
I'M NOT FINE
I'M NOT OKAYI'M NOT OKAYI'M NOT OKAYI'M NOT OKAY

THAT WITCH DOESN'T MATTER TO ME
SHE DOESN'T HURT ME
SHE DOESN'T

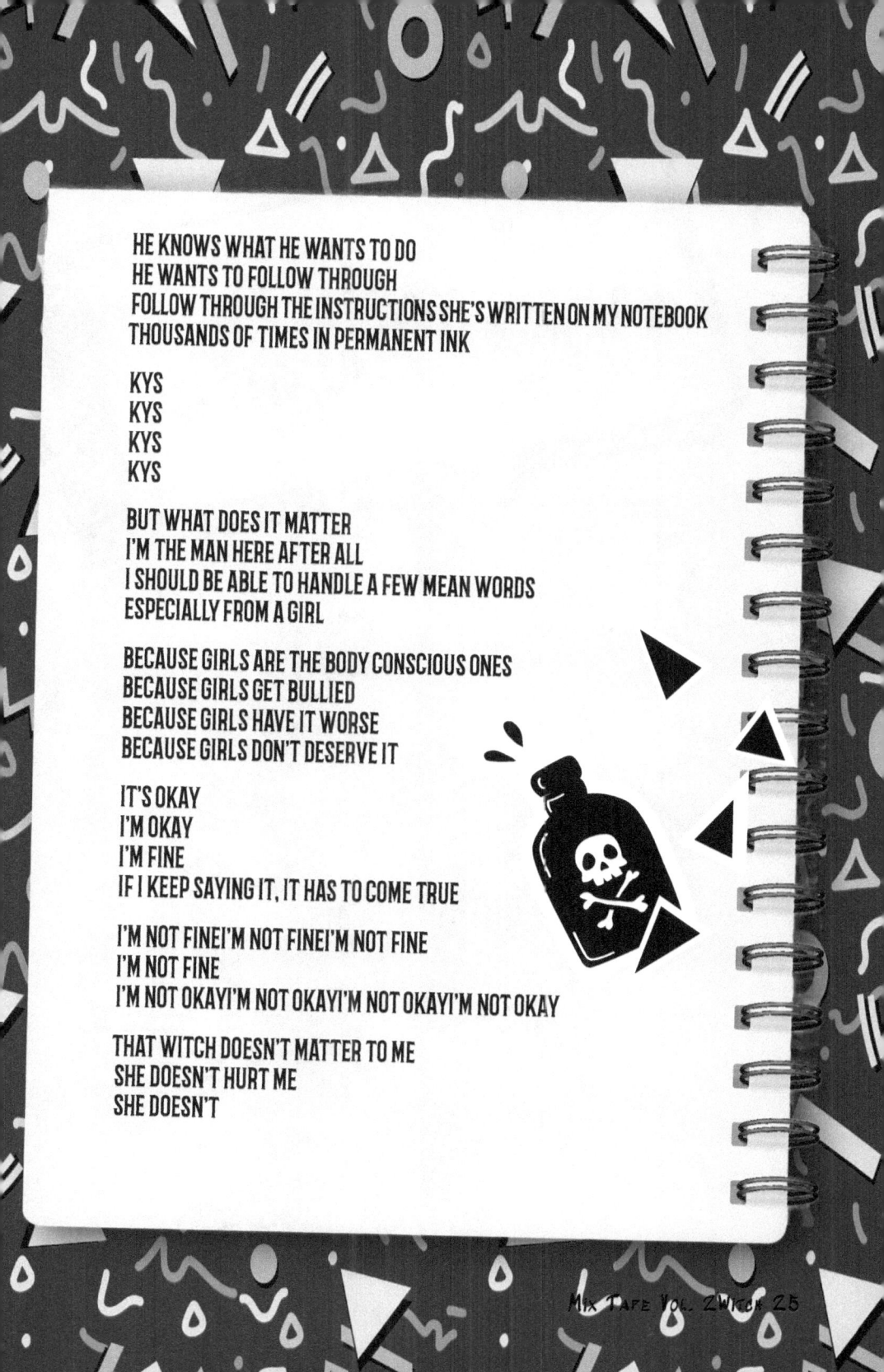

Teen Anguish

Date: 2014

The old me

Who you were then: I was scared and hopeless even though I felt *POWERFUL*. I was in a car accident that left me with severe back injurys resulting in my introduction into the big pharma scene. I was depressed started using other drugs to cope with the mental aspect of the pain and to still help the physical aspect. Started getting in with the wrong crowd made me feel even more hopless and **opened my eyes** to the darker things in life and ultimately poetry saved me when I didn't want to be saved

The NEW me!

Who you are now: I'm a **SURVIVOR** of a 3 year abusive relationship. Now thriving with a man that treats me like gold. I'm still healing I think I'll always be. I've had surgery and my back damage is still declining as well as having fibromyalgia my daily life is still laced with pain but feels like it's finally worth living anyway. Still struggling with depression and PTSD but have a solid grip on it and my passion has always been writing and I want to finally pursue my *dreams* of getting published and sharing my journey to help others feel not so alone

Their is beauty where death resins

When I die I ask you please don't bury me; place me on display for the world to see, once and for all finally stripping me free of my humanity. I want you to skin my flesh and let my insides rain out till my spirit breaks free. Bleaching my bones to make my skeleton a canvas for the world to see. Lacing my skull with hanging vines of green so you can watch them swing with every passing breeze like my thoughts once did before I seized to breathe. My eye sockets will be replace by two tiny mirrors, one for the sun and the moon to reflect the light I once seen and the other is for you to see a piece of yourself inside of me. Pouring out of my ears will be water representing all of the tears I've shed over the years that no one got to see; from the words of musicians and their songs I once loved and heard so clearly . My nose and mouth shall be kept clean for I was never a fan of most smells or talking. Restricting prying hands from where my heart once beat will be thorns guarding my chest cavity. With red roses rooted deep; My love for you will be free to bloom for the rest of eternity. My arms will be lined with feathers from the most beautiful bird's i've ever seen so I can finally fly in my dreams. My hands will be placed in front of me; cupped touching one another like a bum, but instead of being a beggar I'll be making a donation to all the starving critters and In my palms there will be an overflowing abundance of nuts, Berries and seeds for them too help themselves to some food to eat. Planting flowers along my spine I will be filled with vibrant shades of yellow, orange, blue, purple, and pink all of different sizes and shapes will be woven threw my rib cage so people can smile instead of cringe when they look at me. I will restore my purity and Pearls will be draped being pinned from hip to hip covering my pelvis with royalty. My legs will be stained in the deepest most darkest shades of red and with razors there will be carved my favorite poems that I have ever read. Rewriting my painful past; I refuse to be ashamed of the scars I once had. upon my feet I shall have anchors place for all the times I wanted to runaway but chose to stay for my family's sake. Last but not least hang me in a fountain with a noose tied around my neck so the water supplied will keep everything alive, growing inside of me; I will be the most beautiful picture of death you have ever seen. When I die I ask you please don't bury me; place me on display for the world to see, once and for all finally stripping me free of my humanity.

Mad Man

Trust has crumbled
promises have been fumbled
And
Respect no longer means a thing

With all the words you've ever spoken
I've seemed to have ran out of tokens

When hope is lost
Fear is what it costs
To see beyond the boundaries
Of this mind boggling holocaust

A river of love
Surrounded by the rustic smell of lust
Is their anyone out there that you can truly trust?

The marks that resign in you skin
They teach you how
But then they attempt to shun you once you've committed a sin

If you ask me where just a bunch of hypocrites
Trying the best we can to make it across
Before these bridges burn to a crisp
With a lighter still in hand
Your fucking insane
A full blown mad man

Earthquake

Death stained beauty ruptures my soul leaving me in a timeless trance behind this wall of flesh; I make people feel the inevitable. behind my eyes I'm filled with gold surrounded by land mines. polluting my mind, stealing my heart, taunting my soul beyond my human control I'm a walking stone. Make to last, never to change as the earth evolves; I shall forever stay the same till the day another's life altered my mistakes. Making me tremble beneath the outskirts of your Canyon; your shaking me deeper into another layer of flawless regret. As tragedy chips away; I'm dealing with my garnished display. Fighting my insanity wondering if I shall ever be sane; why must life be so vain. I'm running thin as my stone life sheds; I've transformed yet again. I look at my reflection only to appear as glass. Shattered to the core I'm cracking to the edge, it won't be long now till I parish. Don't be sac when you cut yourself cleaning up my mess; no human bein has ever been built nor meant to last.

The moon echoed my soul

A cascade of light that overrides your sight
As it sinks deep within the galaxy
consuming the tragedy of forgotten casualties of this centuries lies.
Getting cradled by the midnight void I feel the richest vibes right before the sun rise
But when the darkness sheds
And transforms into light
I tend to lose my sight
Getting blinded by the fight
Of realities endless demise.
I was never any good at saying my good byes
So I'll just say good night
And fade beneath the surface of this everlasting light and if you dare to look above,
searching right before the surface of space
you'll be sure to never miss my face.

Illusions

Seamless illusions ripple the once silky sight of my lake of life as these unspoken words transform into stone just to sink beneath the surface of this metaphoric life. Forbidden to revise or vocalize my drowning rights, I wonder why no one can truly handle what they behold inside their spirituality powered minds. I almost feel as if I'm the only one with a solid grip on this liquid life. Open your eyes, if you where truly happy with your lives you wouldn't feel so threatened by my placid vibes. I'm sick and tired of absorbing your artificial disguise so take it off before you trip one of my underwater mines that will blow you sky high at the sight of an insecure Fisher man's line.

Headache

Silk covered spikes massage my mind to the rhythm of my thoughts barricaded inside this castle of delinquent demise. I feel hopeless but I'm filled with a whole other life, one that will never be able to die. I was built to survive and born to strive so weather or not my life made sense will be left for you to decide. Either way I'm just trying to feel alive in a world full of regret accompanied by promises that no longer mean a thing as you look into the eyes of mankind you can see their souls as our humanity withers away.

Shift shape

Time shifts and shakes leaving me to deal with the ashes that have formed beneath the fallen rubble of this ever lasting earthquake ruining my mind; is their even anything left for me to find ? Maybe my vital signs will 're align and I'll no longer have to wear a disguise because if we where to revise the last couple years of this so called life I'd be the first in line to get baptized; I should probably have more bible verses memorized but I can help to think what if this book is full of lies, I can't even trust my own mind and my eyes can't seem to leave the sky and I can't help but to wonder what really happens when we die? My soul wants to fly and my heart keeps searching for another life to walk within its path; I need someone I can grasp, perhaps I'll just say Fuck it and create my own path one that doesn't involve a modern-day display of my generations dismay, I'm smarter then your average pray; I'm in love with the game and act accordingly to what I'm about to play.

Recovering

I'm not broken nor am I lost I'm simply recovering; I've known myself for far to long. I've grown flowers in my mind even after you've mistaken them for weeds and yanked them out till I went color blind and couldn't produce anymore seeds; leaving me no other choice but to bleed. I've watered my pride but only after I've felt what it's like to be run dry; I should probably tell the drugs goodbye but they keep me sane when all I've ever wanted was to die. My eyes are a wishing well that will catch you by surprise making your wallet shrink as your soul grows in size; I'm not digging for gold. my heart has always been rich, besides i've always been a hopeless romantic; falling in love with anything money can't buy. Going with flow and chasing the tide till I fell to my knees and howled at the midnight sky. I don't want you to tell me that everything will be alright, I need you by my side and to tell me that it's fine if you don't know what you want out of this life.

Natural disaster

I feel as if theirs a silent earthquake erupting before me as I watch the ground I once stood upon begin to separate dispersing my foundation that slubbers; dragging me beneath the ruins I once beheld and cherished so dearly till it became a part of me. Now I find my self descending once again teeter totting between what I want and what I know i must do to survive. Their will never be enough words to enlighten you, making you fully comprehend this natural apocalypse that ignites my vessel into feeling belittled once again. As I unleash my emotions before you I grab a hold of myself rubbing my magic wings, calling my guardian angles to come forth but they don't appear; they must not be listening. For they're no where to be found, no where to be seen and all I can think is; if only these wings where a lamp and my angles where genies; Maybe then they would of graced me, making me believe once again while they caress my warm blooded bein to feel alive like I so dearly crave to be. I'm losing my mind as my body falls getting swallowed by the crevices that grew beneath my feet. Just know that I will never give up, I keep trying to find solid ground but it cannot be found living in this land. This world was made for you, not for me but that doesn't necessarily mean that it hasn't evolved; Wrapping around me, embedding me into different realms of reality and I can't escape for it's growth has bonded me, smothering me, making it harder for me to breath everyday feeling as if their has been weights laid upon my cheat making the air escaping from my lungs a combination of heavy, sharp, shallow and deep till it feels as if theirs no more oxygen left to inhale or release. Why must this world keep doing this to me?

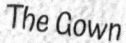

The Gown

I wear a gown; a cascade of rainbows and thunder clouds drift around with bitter glitter sprinkling down. I'm royalty without a crown waiting to be Buried 6ft underground.

I wear a gown; it's almost like an invisible cloak you have to get close enough to see what's really hidden underneath. Don't get to close or you might get a glimpse of this psychological apocalypse.

I wear a gown; That drapes down covering my razor kissed hips from all of you fucking hypocrites.

I wear a gown; Filled with holes and gray stains from all the cigarettes I puffed away.

I wear a gown; That never asked to we worn but I still put it on and strapped it tight now I can't breath and I'm losing sight.

Freedom

with opened eyes and a dagger in my hand I'll carve my name into another land. Rising above as you place me in a casket I'll be smothered by the warmth greater then my favorite jacket. Reaching evaluation at its final resolution I'll be reunited with all my misplaced emotions. traveling threw out time and space I'll finally find my happy place.

Empty Heart

I'm an empty heart so fill me with your sweet tears I need to be replenished with something before I whither into thin air. You follow me not far behind who I once was trying to get a grasp on me; I'm not quite sure how you manage to stay pumping. Producing a steady beat when I feel as if you where losing speed, you never fail to amaze me. You stumbled upon places filled with people I never wanted to meet and worst of all you let them be apart of you before you even took the time to discuss it with me. Now I'm sitting here getting sick and tired of having to constantly chose between keeping or cutting you loose; I'll forever be torn between loving and hating you.

Cast Away

My bones break with every silent escape I fall deeper into a world full of mistakes mocking my every move like a predatory snake. I'm walking the plank with a mysterious face for I never really felt a connection to this place. I stair at you then glance down at the threshing waves craving to rid this place of another dying breed. Without saying a word or twitching my face I fall to my knees; ready to kiss the sea I'm finally escaping my warm blooded being for I've always loved the way ice cold winds bind me.

Lost

Empty waves of regret Ruffles my primitive mind till I think again, once more, till it becomes a chore; no one knows what's happening behind the Scenes of another humans reality. Lagging behind one of a kind; I'm losing my mind. How could one compare? You cant. it's not fair. I'm ready to put an end to this gruelling despair gravitating around me as I struggle to inhale air I can't find myself anywhere. Where am I? What's going on? Who's all even here?

Silent screams

Swinging thoughts alter my emotions as I walk down this path paved with unspoken devotion. screaming as loud as I can but no one can hear for I am drowning on all these silent tears cascading around my hollow frontier.

Haunted

digging myself in and out of this grave theirs no such thing as a normal way to behave. I can hear the sounds of crows while I disassemble the bones of the skeletons you've once planted in my soul, they never seize to grow. it's almost as if they can regenerate; replacing their brittle broken bones back into place I swear they get stronger the more that I break. Day after day I toss and turn trying to sort threw these memories but I always seem to find my self in the same place. forever living life in a timeless daze. I can feel my emotions as they rise and decay never stopping to maintain a spot in the same place. I guess this is the life I have made. I wouldn't wish this upon anyone else. God bless you all. I hope you have a wonderful day.

When You Know

Date: 2017

The old me

Who you were then: I was 19, so only just barely still a teenager. I had been struggling with **severe suicidal** ideations when I was 18, so this was me processing all that on paper.

Who you are now: **Therapy** is a wonderful thing, and so is recognizing that life doesn't need to be taken so seriously. Things are better now.

The NEW me!

When you know
That you have no **SOUL**
You lost that part
When you were 18 years old.

Cover the hole
Pulling the edges
Nobody told you
There would be dredges.
STEPPING on air

Look at the streetlights
Thinking about all
The 'MIGHT NOT'S and 'MIGHT'S

Stepping on stone
Cursing your breathing
Imploding **EXPLODING**
Internal seething

Nobody watches
Out for the day
When the eclipse starts
And *BREAKING* ropes fray

Faces in shadows
Movement in mirror
Hoping that someday
The world will seem clearer

Date: 2018

Who you were then: I was a senior in high school, going through what I felt was an immense change, through schooling life, friends, work, and other **growing pains**. It was a time in which I never seemed to feel happy or feel enjoyment in my daily life, constantly questioning my worth and what my *future* would hold.

The old me

The NEW me!

Who you are now: Now, as a senior in university, I've become a result of these changes and have found a **SOLID FOOTING** in where I stand in my life. I've become a person I'm proud of and have grown up. Still using writing as a way to alleviate my stress and my worries, I've done a lot of reflecting and thought I'd like to share some of my past thoughts with the **FUTURE GENERATION** in hopes that they may relate or find comfort in my words.

10:26 pm

why is it that we are constantly chasing happiness?
pushing ourselves to our absolute limits
but never seeming to be in reach
as if it is merely a figment of our imagination
an oasis of our mind
when in reality happiness should be a constant
a state of being in which we may flow in and out of
but is always present.
how unruly is it we feel that we are purposed to find happiness as our end goal

"i just want to be happy"
"i want to find happiness"

how tragic
how heartbreaking
that we are born into a sadness
with only dreams of happiness

- still, i hope to find you|

HEARTSTRINGS?

Date: 2018

Who you were then: I was in my freshman year of college, ~~depressed~~ and trying to find out who I was. I always felt like I was physically **DROWNING** in anxiety, so I wrote this about that feeling.

The old me

Who you are now: Today, I am working as a nurse and living with the **LOVE** of my life! I can't be HAPPIER that I experienced the angst that I did because it made me **stronger**, and I would not change it if I could.

The NEW me!

> Today I felt like giving up.
> I'm swimming through thick muggy water
> and barely able
> to keep my head above it.
> I'm constantly exhausted,
> strung out.
> I don't know who I am at my core
> and I feel like I don't have time to find out.
> I am literally clawing
> at my head
> at all times
> trying to swim but in the process
> cutting everything open and bleeding out.
> I want him to turn around and rub my back innocently,
> I want a big drink of cold water and to force
> cold air down my nose until there's
> no fog left inside my lungs.
> I want the sticky cobwebs pulled from the back of me
> and a string to connect my heart to my head,
> so I can finally know who I am.

Mix Tape Vol. 2 Heartstrings? 39

DIARY

Date: Late 2018-early 2019

Who you were then: I was 17 years old by the end of 2018. I stopped playing for two soccer teams after more than 10 years at 16 years old due to a torn ACL and I was staying home after school most days because I finally had the time to relax in bed. I've had major anxiety all throughout it my life but playing soccer helped me ignore all my feelings so a year into no more soccer I had time to listen to my feelings and soon became depressed. I thought the anxiety would go away as I got older but it just got worse. I spent a lot of time in bed thinking and overthinking and writing in the notes app of my phone. I was also smoking weed regularly and went through major psychological withdraw every time I ran out because i was too scared to get a job that would allow a stead income. I didn't actually realize I was depressed, you'll read about how my best friend told me I was depressed and how I came to terms with that.

Who you are now: Today I'm somewhat in the same position. I went to college and dropped out after 3 years because I couldn't handle my social anxiety. Now I'm in therapy trying to get help. I still smoke a lot and still have no job because I'm terrified of how my mental health will be affected once go to a job that only have because I need money. I hate money. But other than that I have a much better understanding of the chemicals and how they work in my brain.

Understanding MS

1 in every 25 people are **sociopaths**. That involves having less empathy than one should. That may be the reason not everyone is nice. For that one in twenty five, they only think of themselves while the rest of us question what is wrong with some people's lack in perception on being nice to others

One of my greatest sins, is my minds consumption of media. When I take my dogs out at night I look up at the infinite space between me and the sky. The beauty of the moon and stars are out and I cannot contain my complete astonishment for *space* and NATURE. They bring natural emotions out for me. Media has a temporary hold on me.

I am consumed in myself, but as a 17 yo girl in the 21st century, it's not in the way you think. I stopped posting pictures on Instagram 2 years ago. I went from a **600 day streaks** to snapping one person maybe once a day/week. I no longer looks for other people's approval through social media. I take advantage of the internet and figure out exactly who I am as a person for my own knowledge, because I am all who will matter in the long run.

I don't understand the use of small talk for myself. I see how it helps others in a way but with the right person I like to talk on a **deeper**, more *meaningful* level. And that is why people take me as a quiet person, when really I let myself pick and choose who can handle a real conversations I am looking for. I have found very few fitting for these talks.

I am always in my head. I can **DAYDREAM** for a whole day. Talking does not come easy to me but when I am with myself, I have thoughts tripping over one another.

For the amount of time I spend in my head, there is a lot of clutter built up. I use my notes as a way to organized everything. From favorites to dreams to plans. I just always want to remember anything and everything I feel is remotely important now or will be in the future.

There are very few topics that I could talk on and on about. Knowing a lot about a little. I am going to BROADEN my spectrum. Knowing a little about a lot.

10/1/18

I understand what is going on in my head but I cannot stop it. I feel people have simplified the idea of a demon inside them. The thoughts still sound like me but it's as if they are being taken over by Lucifer himself and I have no control. My conscious has left my body for the time being and I am guided by when feels good but will regret later. I continue with the act as if it's the only way I know. My mind makes common sense out of it.

11/7/18

I've always been so happy and content.

This change coming with being senior and college stuff is wearing me out. I feel like 20 things are changing every day and I don't have **CONTROL** or **STABILITY**.

I've become suicidal for the first time in my life and I feel so weak, like I should be okay it's not that bad but it is

I've had anxiety forever but I've only come to understand it recently and it's increasing everyday

For the past month I've been *smoking weed* and it's made me so calm and even quieter than I already am but it helped.

I've been out for two days and I'm already having horrible breakdowns like when the school year started.

Explaining it to people sucks because saying what's wrong out loud to others makes me feel like it's not a big deal. But I can't just explain why

I'm **breaking down**, this sadness has been manifesting for longer than I can remember each time. The little things pile up and it gets worse and idk what to do.

11/9/18 12:20 am

I have people around me that want to know what's wrong. They actually care to go out of their way to text **Arabelle** and ask about me, check on how I'm feeling a couple times a day, give advice, worry for me.

I should stop feeling insecure about how I look. I hate the "judge a book my it's cover" notion society has set on us.

Beto for PRESIDENT

How the fuck am I supposed to find a senior quote if we can't be inappropriate.

11/14/18 21:34

Instead of studying for a math test, I started a book without finishing the current book I'm on. I want to write a book. The DREAM, the dream is to write a book and I want that to be my career and I will never have to worry about money management bc the book will have brought me enough success that my life is completely stable and I can help others and I can cross off things on my BUCKET LIST easily and be happy that my book helped people and those people helped me and I can continue to help people.

I've kicked my social anxiety to the curb. (After this revelation, I was told I had a presentation to do in school. What a way to truly see how much I conquered my anxiety. I could still feel the claws coming up my throat and the closing sensation to block off words but not until the night bore my presentation. That is growth.) Anxiety is fear and I know that fear is nothing to fear for the opportunity we were given to live is so beautiful and here we are being scared. One day we will all die and so will the people around us and every action we take will not be remembered so live for what you desire and stick to it. Regret nothing that brings you *happiness* and forget the judgement in people's eyes because that look is far too close minded for you.

Every *journey* is unique and without the past to bring us where we are, who would we be.

The past is so telling of a person.

I want to write a book. No dream is too big. My journey starts now.

I'm back at that point where I want to write down every thought I have because I don't want to forget anything.

Kaylin and my mother know me better than I know myself. And I really thought I knew myself, seriously. I should have listened when they said teens are moody and stubborn and are trying to find themselves. All those things were true for me. In a **bubble** thinking I knew everything that was most important to me.

How could I let my anxiety clo se me off to so many things. Job opportunities, **new friends** and relationships, my future. I let my closed off anxiety chose my future. It selected such a secluded path and it didn't allow me to dream big. Only a DISMALLY SHALLOW way of easy living.

The wandering mind.

Let art influence more art. A Truly beautiful chain effect.

11/21/18 16:45

I shaved my head this past Sunday and I think it put my anxiety back to square one. I guess we'll see when I go to Lizzie's house for *Friendsgiving*. I want to be okay, I control it, it does not control me.

Honey, it's alright - Greg Alan isavok

11/26/18

Autry brought weed and smoked in the GARAGE and got caught. I took some off him when he left and now I'm back to my high ways.

I have school tomorrow

I still really want to write a book.

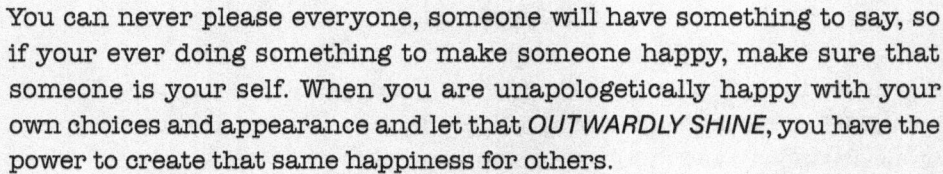

11/29/18

You can never please everyone, someone will have something to say, so if your ever doing something to make someone happy, make sure that someone is your self. When you are unapologetically happy with your own choices and appearance and let that *OUTWARDLY SHINE*, you have the power to create that same happiness for others.

I want to try the 16/8 fasting thing starting tomorrow bc tonight I may drinkkkk.

I am so grateful for Kaylin. Her opening up to me about her past brought us so much **closer** and it took away my doubts of if we should even be friends bc at the beginning on the year I felt like we couldn't hold a conversation anymore. I came to learn that she was focused on a guy and that's okay but it limited what she could talk about since it was on her mind so much. This same *situation* happened in a book I just read and I'm glad to know that we will be okay.

I feel like I find my **true friends** through my minimal judgement perspective. The human person is so complex that judgement is too simple of an act to succumb to. The people in my life are there for a reason, on each of our parts to say, you are my favorite among the millions of others out there.

Manipulating my mind is my favorite. From my childhood to now I have convinced myself to see outside of the societal standards. I have cut down majorly on judging others, told myself I was beautiful until I believed it bc I definitely didn't when I started, wear what clothing I want to and not what everyone else says I should. Be happy with myself in any form I come in bc this life we are given is more beautiful than nature itself. Honestly with the help of **YouTube** and other amazing weird people of this world I have become a person I didn't know I always wanted to be.

nurture
- yes theory
- Jenna marbles
- Yousef erikat
- Billy eilish
- Supernatural
- Misha Collins
- Jaded Padalecki
- Jensen Ackles
- Prince EA
- Ted talks
- Ben Stiller
- Alice in wonderland
- Sia
- Tom syndicate
- Soccer
- Will Smith
- J Cole
- Brenden urie

11/30/18 23:37

I really have lived a crazy fortunate life. I feel like I haven't experienced a single outstanding trauma in my 17 years. I learn more and more about my friends past and then getting beat, unnecessary verbal abuse, losing a major *loved one*, being in really shit relationships and cutting and suicidal and depression and insecurities. And for them it's just normal shit that happened. Why am I so lucky, I want to cry for all of them, each and every person deserves to be happy with who they are and live in a **safe environment**. I wish more people could see how amazing they are without even trying, and when they do try it's a beauty.

MIX TAPE VOL. 2 DIARY 47

That reminds me why social media is such a dangerous game. People post the best of their lives. My friends have so much money but with the traumatic life they lived, it doesn't seem worth it. It's like, "you were beat by your parents bc they thought that's the best way to discipline you," but that really leaves horrible mental SCARS that they have to live with for the rest of their life.

The older generations are such a **heartless** scary group of individuals. I really hope for the life of me that our generation brings light to the deep wretched hole of empathetic-less people.

12/6/18 14:13

I hate *wasting* my breath with unnecessary words

I feel like the first verse in love of my life by *queen*

12/7/18 20:55

Kaylin's grandmother passed away and I love Kaylin so much that it *hurts* me knowing she has to go through this. Like she can't catch a fucking break. I really love her that it hurts. I just love her.

I don't even have to say it out loud so get a million **CHILLS** down my back. Just thinking about it makes me at ease.

It probably won't ever happen. She has Brian and i just want her to be happy. I don't think I could give her everything she would want in a relationship but I sure as hell know she can give me *everything*. She already has. That's selfish though and I want more than anything for her to be happy over me.

- Star

12/8/18 12:41

I'm out of delaying ingredients but it's not that bad. I'm just lonely and I feel like I **NEED** human contact. Just the touch of someone else. I keep reading ao3 but I think it's only making it worse. I know I wrote before that I like to "feel" my feelings but right know I want the act on my feelings and not make them stronger bc I'm going to burst.

13:01

God I need to DISTRACT myself before my mind wonders to the best and easiest way to get weed of someone. Idk if I can hold myself over all day.

13:47

I don't ever think I have wrote about my *future husband / wife*. I miss them already if that's possible. I don't think I've met them yet. I want to feel like I know it's them when the time come. I've never really experienced being in a real relationship but I ready miss the early mornings with them cuddled around me and the peaceful silent moments and when I can just look at the sleep. Standing back and watch them talk to my family, going to sleep with them at night, post sex glow of happiness, feel their *heart beat* and the sound of them breathing, their laugh and smile. Their eyes... I just want to look at them in the eyes non stop. I want the words love to truly mean something. I feel like I only understand 1/4 of the word love.

I didn't realize I've been pushing almost every new person in my life away. I'm just too scared to try to have a relationship if I don't feel the connection almost right away. Idk if I can ever just give people a chance. 3 guys I've pushed away and at the time I thought it was just because I didn't feel the connection but I know see that I was avoiding trying to push for a real relationship. I want it to be easy but it isn't.

I got so lucky with Colin. But then I was a fucking DIPSHIT and broke up with him. Why the fuck did I do that?, I know why, I'm a piece of shit that's why. I could have been so happy with him. SO HAPPY I know it, THATS IT, one of those people I knew it was going to be great bc the connection was naturally beautiful that it makes me want to cry. I lost it. Him.

I can by happy with him, he has a girlfriend, he probably won't leave her especially since I shaved my head. Also that's mean, I don't want to try to steel him away from her. That's just causing problems in their lives and I just hope the **UNIVERSE** puts us in each others paths again in life.

Engeli is super nice and I could tell through his music that he is humble and down to earth. **Bright soul**. I feel bad for not talking to him anymore.

14:14

This is all my withdraw phase, I can feel it in my chest, the weight and all the feelings that come with it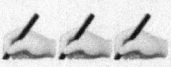

15:41

Powder and where you gonna go by Gregory Alan isokov

17:19

These **EMOTIONS** are really hitting me like a truck

Kaylin said I don't really share my feelings and she's right, I hope that doesn't ruin anything, I guess it would have already if it was a big enough problem for her or it will cause something in the future.
What I want to share with her:
-The **CHOKING** feeling I have
-I want to be with someone so bad I could cry about it and never stop, I'm consumed in being alone and I'm starting to feel the real effects of loneliness
-I think I was ready to be more open to talking to people. then I shaved my head and I sometimes think people won't even try talking to be bc of appearance.
like I'm missing out on that person bc they

are having a hard time figuring out why I was so weird as to shave my head. But I also say idgaf what people say but my appearance has never been a problem until now. I want to say that then I guess that person shouldn't be in my life if they don't want to talk to me just bc if my hair.
That's not true though. I've had more people than ever talking to me about my hair. I just feel like I cut any ties I could have with guys bc they don't like how I look like them. *OBVIOUSLY* our shy little Wyo provides me with zero girls so my literal dyke haircut has brought me no benefits in my finding a relationship with anyone.

Idk what to do

20:43

Somebody to love by queen
In a, I'm **drunk** and I just want somebody but like a tipsy happy drunk way bc the song is upbeat I guess

12/9/18

Did I want him back or just the thought of him back. Idkkkkk

Hopefully the need is gone, I feel a lot better today.

I really need to stop drinking, compared to weed if just fucking sucks

12/15/18 18:30

I crave **intimacy** so much but I cannot find it. I've stopped looking. I can no longer jump into people for them to disappoint me. For those who I do have around, they have intimacy with others, I am just the friend.

No matter what time of day it is I'm growing sadder to be alone. Accompanied by a anxious ROCK, I just want to shared what's going on in me without feeling locked.

MIX TAPE VOL. 2 DIARY 51

I think I want to go to millersville more

I listen to everyone else's problems but I don't how to share my own. Even with Kaylin on the phone, knowing I'm sad, I don't know what to say. I just shut her down. SHUT MYSELF DOWN.

I don't force anyone to tell me anything bc it's not my place. Maybe with Kaylin it is my place, if that makes sense. I feel like the only way for her to get anything out of me is for her to force me to talk with me **breaking** down crying with no where else to go but just say the shit I feel. I say idk why I'm sad but wtf. I know why, it's fucking written above at 18:30. I'm just sad to have people who want to help and idk how to give in.

Yesterday I was sad after taking about Tito with Kay. I fell asleep then to avoid the feelings. As soon as I woke up I went to a HOCKEY GAME to further avoid them. Then Kay brought up alcohol and I suggested weed and then all night I was with friends slightly less sad and high. Now I'm just alone on a Saturday crying by myself. Nothing's helping on my phone, no SM, YouTube, Millersville tour. Will talking really help. I guess if writing it out is somewhat helping barely then talking to another person, the right person, will help. I just don't know who that person is. Wish I could say Kay but then we'd still be on the phone and I'd be crying to her about how drained I am.

I know what it feels like to have so much good in life but still be sad. And then be sad that I can't just be *grateful* and **HAPPY**.

12/18/18 04:49

Kaylin has literally never had it easy, in any part of her life. She's had the most rough life and I'm happy to be here for her. I'd be nowhere else beside next to her. I can never not be friends with her. Hopefully we're a forever thing.

12/18/18 23:19

Kay is going through a really bad time right now. I want to pick her up Dunkin for breakfast. Anything to help her out. Today I brought her a brownie, **Oreos**, and a cookie and cream pop tart. Food is only temporary happiness but it's better than nothing when you can't find any happiness. She'll make it through. I'll *FIGHT* any and every second of the day for her even when and especially when she's too tired to fight for herself. Life is so cruel but I was put on Kay's path for a reason and I'm so grateful for the bright friendship we have.

12/19/18

I'm 60% sad and all my friends are sad and I feel like I'm being a bad friend bc I don't know how to help them.

For the lest two days I've been out of the house doing shit and coming home at night and falling **asleep** right away. Today I finally got to be in bed and my mom come in my mom and yelled at me for the mess and for being lazy and to stop sleeping and I just want to relax. I really thought I could get away with not crying today but she got me. Moment she left I felt the tears dampen my cover and I just laid their listening to Gregory Alan.

I just want Kaylin to be happy and find someone who she truly *deserves* to be with, Dylan to be able to sleep and recover from every physical injury she has, the peace of mind that Sophia will make it past 25. That all of them to make it past 25.

I'm so tired

I want to be able to talk to someone about everything. I can't go to anyone. I want a therapist.

12/21/18 11:48

Where you gonna go by Gregory Alan

Misha can really have perfect timing sometimes - insta poem

Honey it's alright by Gregory Alan

20:35

The first time I slept so I didnt have to be awake. So I didn't have to deal with being alone. Waking up SWEATING and sadder than when I was previously awake sucks.

21:04

What's wrong with me

23:10

I DONT NEED IT
IT WILL MAKE IT WORSE
I DONT NEED IT
IT WILL MAKE IT WORSE
I DONT NEED IT
IT WILL MAKE IT WOSRE
I DONT NEED IT
IT WILL MAKE IT WORSE
I DONT NEED IT
IT WILL MAKE IT WORSE

23:17

It's okay
You'll be okay
It's okay
You'll be okay

12/22/18 15:07

Kaylin will be okay bc I'll will NEVER leave her side, I'll make sure she'll always end up okay.

12/23/18 21:28

How could my feelings change so fast.
I don't even want to see her tomorrow for church.

I'm a shit friend, she deserves someone better. Fuck me I'm really shit, how can I not even be there for her.

She really just **DRAGGED ME DOWN** with her but I cut her loose and if sometime happens tonight then I will never forgive myself.

She told me that I was the only reason she stayed alive and I just told her I couldn't talk anymore after she said she really doesn't care anymore. I was being selfish after she was selfish and didn't consider that I couldn't take shit talk, especially this late, "Mama they're mating at night."

I can't do this anymore

I don't even want to go through the last half a year to *graduate*, I just wanna be done. I don't want any of it.

I just want to get high off my ass on NYE
and then I want it all to go away, everything.

Two depressed friends can't help each other. They'll only make it WORSE

12/24/18 05:19

I apologized to Kay at 03:41 and i really hate how much I sound in it. I can just picture in my head how much I sound like Brian or any other guy saying sorry after being a dickhead. I really do want to go to church with her today and I just want everything to be okay again.

1/1/19 19:40

I uh, got a hold of Autry's 💎 and took some like 5 times and it started on the 26 and I used the last of it today.

I also smoked with trace once in his grandmothers house 🖕🖕 a couple nights ago, Jackson is hilarious and like a puppy, he's a junior and I think Alex is a senior or something bc his gf is a sophomore

It's only been 5 hours but I can feel the heaviness and deep rutting weighing in my chest

1/8/19 18:13

How am I supposed to go and talk to these people about how much I hate public speaking and my anxiety when my anxiety is making me too **EMOTIONAL** to even get a word out. Go talk to people about how you have a horrible time talking to people about your problems. Wtf. I want them to understand my problem but half the problem is is I literally don't want to talk. Can I just become a mute. I do t want to talk anymore to anyone. I just wanna write. I'm literally wiping away tears just writing this itself.

God I feel pathetic.

The problem with saying THIS WILL PASS is that for it to pass I have to go through it and going through it is what is killing me.

1/10/19 09:41

Love you bub, grateful you no longer have to suffer

This girl in front of me asked what I would do to improve my life. It's such a *genuine question* and I wasn't expecting it. I said I would get rid of my anxiety. She asked how would I do that, without pills, if I could have something imaginary, what could I have to help myself. Idk and I wish I know.

Smoking won't help that's for sure, it'll only make it worse when I'm out. It'll suppress these agonizing feelings and they will come back stronger than before.

I just want that temporary release. I'm **CRAVING** it. It forget everything. It's so much. Mentally crippling.

She said my answer helped her and left. She's a new student.

NVM she's back 🖕

20:03

I have this way of finding great people/things that inspire me when I am at my lowest or my lowest is coming. It's like I'm getting ready for the fall back and soon new spotlight focus of my life.

Soccer-> *supernatural*>conventions-> my love for Misha Jared and Jensen

Started reading more
    In-depth understanding of myself
      Learn more through the access of internet
        Music

          I'm allowing myself to be inspired by the great **weird** creative people of today and the past

            22:28

              How emotions can change in a matter of days hours minutes moments... a beautiful and *scary* thing

23:04

I get anxious when I am sharing something I didn't ever expect to be read my any eyes but my own. Only one person holds that title of seeing my **TRUE THOUGHTS**. It's odd to let someone in on your bizarre weirdness/madness. Oh but madness in a good way.

1/11/19 09:17

I'm going crazy, madness in a bad way. KAYLIN REWLLY DOESNT WANT TO TWLK ABOIT WHAT SHE TEXT ME. I'm so *confused*. I'm literally running wild in my head.

22:05

Dylan has my hopes up and it's **SCARING** me. I can't help it at this point. I know what I want. I just hope when the time come that it is reciprocated. I can feel myself fall asleep drunkenly to the thought of her. No alc necessary.

KG 1/14/19

With little support how can one lean on another. Too much trust was put into her. ~~Hypocrisy~~ stings when to come from that one person. Is it that hard to earn words of encouragement? I know my truth and what's happening to me so why bash on that and lower my ability to grow past what is hurting me. Why can't she be for me what I am for her. Negativity lives in her and I'm not sure if I can live with that.

These new feelings are destroying me.

1/15/19 22:22

The wandering mind can be dangerous. Locked in your head will lead to an unnecessary amount of anxiety. It is easier to stay **silent** but worth the time to talk about it.

1/16/19 19:47

Kaylin won't talk to me about shit.

Dylan is in constant panic attacks and I'm not a fucking therapist. I don't know how to help her. I CONTINUOUSLY search for ways to help people get through their fucking problems.

I just need Kaylin to say fucking anything. I need to know the problem so we can FUCKING fix it. She's just staying silent and it's actually killing me. 6 YEARS AND WE WILL MAKE IT THROUGH THIS IF IT KILLS ME. She could turn out to be so toxic for me but I DONT GIVE A FUCK. I WILL GET HER TO OPEN UP ABOUT THE REAL ISSUES SHES HAVING BC I DINT WANT ANYONE ELSE. This relationship we have is too important. It's not something I will ever give up on. We're in too deep.

As for Dylan. I DONT KNOW WHAT TO DO.

1/17/19 07:50

I'm taking it all in, every detail. The way our legs are crossed away from each other. How we aren't talking or even trying. Heads in other tasks. Your back almost facing me fully. Like a divide I can't get myself to break because I feel like you don't want that. So different from how we were during Christmas. My stomach is sick.

08:45

It's hard for me to *understand*. And I love understanding. Getting the facts, details, reasons. Building the foundation to comprehension. That come with words. Spoken outwardly to one another. Knowing, can fix situation. Silence can break them. I can be the other way around sometimes but I do not think that's how it is this time. I've broken down because I couldn't understand how to just say what was needed to be said. That was a battle with myself. It was easier to fix that. When **BATTLING** with another it is more difficult. The human mind is complicated beyond almost everyone's comprehension. Mixing two could be easier; If people could to say what they mean and talk it out with the intention to learn from what is being said. How can you get through to someone who is locked in their own silence, who wishes to ignore the problem. The affect it has on a relationship is destructive. The slow progression of this distraction is torture. I can feel it coming and I just want to fix it but we're stuck. I can't live in the state of torment much longer.

1/17/19 12:20

I talked to Kaylin. I was already in west reading so I called her and asked her to come out to the car.

I left her there and she blew my mind. I need to step back and seriously take in what we talked about. She was right about everything. I can't even understand it. My isolation is actually **KILLING ME**. I need to stay active and connect with other people and limit how much free time I have. Doing nothing and just filling the time with **MEANINGLESS** scrolling through my phone is what I have to change. There is really something wrong with the way I handled 2018. I was never actually fine or okay but I thought I was. Being in my head alone was the torture. I've always dismissed people telling me that I need to be involved and do things with school and spend time outside of being in bed. They must have known. With my single perspective my brain ran through *scenarios* and things that didn't make sense but I made sense of them. I am so locked in my comfort zone.

It's crazy how I would have never been able to make these *connections* without Kaylin. I just not happy and she showed me that.

I could go through *everything* I've been writing down for the past 3 months and pick out instances where I didn't take my own advice. Where I Projected my problems onto other

people. Where I would just sound completely CRAZY. I'm actually kinda scared to go through it.

I just need to find *something* to do.

1/31/19 17:36

I'm **suffocating** again and what I think my only way out of it is avoiding it until it goes away.

Where you gonna go - Gregory

Emails to Myself

Datet: 2018-2019

The old me

Who you were then: Looking back at these **emails** i sent to myself, I had a lot of late night thoughts. 7th grade was my downfall year for some reason. I was definitely a little OVER DRAMATIC but i'm nothing like that now.

The NEW me!

Who you are now: Now, I understand how to maturely go about problems and don't **email** myself instead of speaking up.

Aug 17, 2018, 10:32 PM

hey. i know you're stressed, i can feel it because i am you and that's how we are. people have been talking lately so hopefully you've grown enough tits to shut that down by the time u see this. don't let anyone make you feel unwanted or not special because i love how we are right now and if people can't accept that then screw those fake bitches ALL OF THEM. so my friends who are supposed to be my best friends above all say that "i flirt with every boy" like what the hell am i not allowed to make people feel happy when they're having a bad day?? i just wanna say screw you for thinking that, anyways, do u still have a thing with Jack? he told me he loved me and that i can't tell anyone, but i'm telling you so shhhh. it's sad that i'm talking to myself but i can't say anything to anyone else because i don't trust anyone.

from your cheesy 7th grade self,
you

Sep 14, 2019, 10:40 PM

Hey past me. You're not a thing with James still. He ended everything, hung out other girls all the time which messed u up big time. You miss jack but he clearly doesn't miss you. He doesn't talk to you. He only talks when you're with a prettier friend. You're best friends with Gabby and Isabelle and you've drifted away from Lily and Grace and Sophia because they've had numerous parties without you and you're sick of it. Dance, kickline and school have become the first priority's. Right now kinda sucks but hopefully it gets a little better.

Track 11
Kaley C

UNTITLED

Date: January 2019

The old me

Who you were then: This was about the middle of my junior year of high school. I was having a lot of *anxiety* about my friends, and I felt like I constantly had to impress them and watch how I acted, lest they **ABANDON ME**. I was also in the middle of some really heavy AP courses, so my stress levels were a little crazy. Writing poetry helped my mind stop *spinning* at night and gave me a much-needed outlet.

Who you are now: I still have a lot of the same traits - they're just subdued and better **CONTROLLED**. I'm still a writer, but I'm working my way through college, now. A lot of my angst was small-town drama, and leaving the small town seems to have helped. Those years taught me one really important lesson: choosing to impress others over being true to yourself will only make you *MISERABLE*.

The NEW me!

Silence, I find, hides a great many things.
It hides secrets, for sure.
It hides people, too.
It hides monsters.
It hides contentment.
It hides distractions.

It hides truths you didn't want to know.

It hid me, a few times.

It hid my fear, for I did not want to face it myself.
It hid my anger, for I did not want to hurt you.
It hid my pain, for I did not want you to know.
It hid my knowledge, for I did not want to seem crass.

It hides me, when I refuse to demand an apology.
If I cried they would know me.
They would know I'm different.
They would know it hurts.

Would they care that they hurt me?

Silence answers.

JOURNAL ENTRY 64

Date: February 2019

The old me

Who you were then: I was ADDLED, SCRAMBLED, CAST OFF to sea without any sign of shore. I was a fly on the wall, I was quiet in the wrong sort of way. I was trampled. Spread-eagled, I was choked on **SAINT PATRICK'S** Day. I was frightened and in fear sought out comfort or enticement instead of safety in my own skin. I was un uninvited guest at my own dinner party. I yearned for a hearth, a home, a harbor but I couldn't sit still.

Who you are now: I am a **TINKER**. I toy with, mangle the irresistible identity of each word I stumble upon. I am a pathological liar. I have only now found the strength to begin to entertain the concept of telling the truth, my truth. I am tired. Longhand, my only solace. I may not have an axis, but prose breathes life into my quotidian. Notions of identity, solicitude, and flux became slightly less elusive. By attributing words to the *human experience*, I am granted the false impression that I may begin to comprehend it and perhaps understand my own mind. That very well could be another lie, but I hope not. I am an optimist at heart.

The NEW me!

As a (young) child I spluttered, practically blundered my way through any sort of discussion. I was a bull in the china shop of conversation. In late May 2005, my father left the home and I lost my mother to her own compulsions. It was as if the world had been ~~split~~ splintered into smithereens overnight and yet there I was trudging through the rubble, attempting to make sense of my new reality.*

To speak? Impossible.

And so, I traversed my quotidian in blinks, murmuring incantations sometimes, othertimes |blathering| nonsense. when I opened my throat my naive voice crackled like radio static. — rep!
(I) was incomprehensible. and (yet) when (I) sang, or, rather, when I was onstage, (I) enunciated, I beamed, my words rang true. To be a character, to be other, stripped of any obligation to myself was a relief.

In performance, I found a harbor.

* enough of the rhet. q's

I did not recognize the inherent danger in this, how could I? I was nubile and downy and timorous. I eventually regained my ability to speak and my stutter all but dissipated into a distant memory, but I never ceased to perform. [as a] performer I was perceived [as a] tenacious beast, ravenous and ready to (suck) [took?] the marrow from every bone I came across. In my own skin I suffocated. My voice may not even be my own, but then to whom ~~to to~~ does it belong? I am preoccupied by the ordinary, tales of envy, unrequited desires, I fear time like a shadow I cannot shake —

Untitled

Date: 2019

The old me

Who you were then: at the time I was being committed for trying to kill myself at a mental hospital in arizona. I had been in an abusive relationship with my now ex. there were many feeling going on and **poetry** was the only way I could let it out

The NEW me!

Who you are now: now I am a **varsity tennis player** who is off to college in just a few months. i have grown sense this time and have a great family and a BOYFRIEND who loves and supports me through all the troubles i've ever had.

STUCK

And then break
I want to watch you snap
And bleed
Oh how I want to watch you bleed
I want you in pain
Suck excruciating pain
Till you almost go numb
But numb would be too good for you
So I want you to writhe in agony
Just like I did but more
I want so much more pain for you
I hate you so much
And I want my revenge
But I think you'll do it for me
So I'll wait
And I'll watch
As you destroy your life
And I'll sit on the sidelines
Watching and laughing
At the pain you are in
After all you deserve it
After what you did to me
To all the others
You deserve everything horrid in this world
And if karma doesn't get you first
If you don't fuck up enough first
Then I'll make sure the job gets done
Just like you did to me

The ways I think and the ways I wrote never seem to add up
I can think about anything and everything constantly to a point where everything else fades away
And I can write like a mad man and drown out the world with my words and voice all the inner demons I fight with
But the two still manage to never line up
Maybe it's the constant fear
The fear of being judged and labeled
Or maybe it's just that my head and my hand don't connect
And the path is getting cut somewhere
Or maybe it's just me
Being too scared to see
Will force me to see
Just how bad off I am
Just how awful of a person I am
Just how dangerous my words can be
Just how it's my head protecting me from myself
Maybe it's just my head protecting me from myself
Maybe it's a good thing my writing ways and thinking ways never add up

FREE me

I bled so much that night
I watched it drip off my skin
And pool below me
If was nice
Almost therapeutic
But it really wasn't was it
That stunt landed me in a ward
Just for people like me
People who watched themselves bleed
And ate so little
Their bones broke inside them
People who could hear and see more than you and I
People who were broken
And beat
People just like me
And it was there I learned just how broken I am
And man I don't care
I love my cracks
And I think I'll keep them
They survived with me
And if they lived when I didn't
Then I think they can stay

Mix Tape Vol. 2 Untitled 75

I Know

Date: 1/30/20

The old me

Who you were then: At the time of this poem I had an eating disorder. This effected every aspect of my life and even altered my *BRAIN CHEMISTRY*. My parents were trying to help me fight my ED, but I was very resistant in letting them do so.

The NEW me!

Who you are now: Today I am well on my way to **recovery** and really feel like I'm living and enjoying life.

I Know

I know its all in my head
I know I could end up dead
I know the dangers that come with it
It's just so hard to quit this.

I know you are fighting for my life,
But I can't just stop,
 when I've been doing it for so long,
I know you want to help me
All these thoughts I have scare me
Please help me out.

I know I'm going down
And I don't want to drown,
But I'm torn apart
Right from the start
I know I need to stop,
I just can't drop it like a bad habit,
Because part of me still wants to have it.

I know all these things you think I don't understand
I just can't grasp it in my hand,
I know its hard for you to watch me
But its just so hard to stop me.

By: L

Letter to Rendezvous

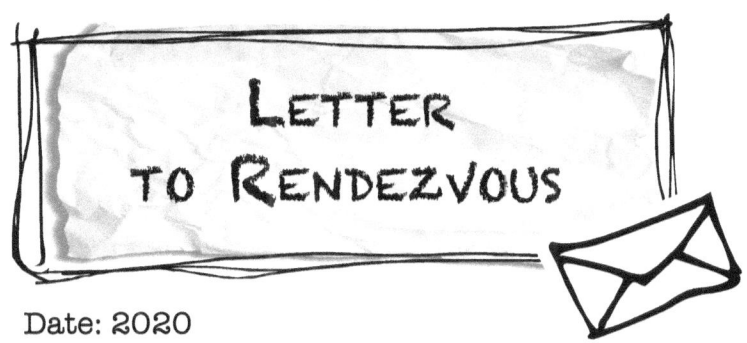

The old me

Date: 2020

Who you were then: Hi, This happened during **COVID** and I was nineteen years old. I was young and I really liked a boy who didn't like me back so I settled for being his friend and it was hard. I couldn't express my **feelings** so I decided to write about it.

The NEW me!

Who you are now: Well I left my country to go study abroad and I'm most definitely over him thank **GOD**. He was important to me and we are still friends.

Date: 22nd March 2020

Dear Rendezvous,

The stars are gone now and I'm sad
But now the darkness of the night reminds me of your eyes
Your dark big beautiful eyes
And how I'll love to stare at them all the time
And marvel at them cause God made them this beautiful
I love the way the thought of you makes my heart skip a beat
It's exciting and beautiful but at the same time it annoys me
You don't seem to be leaving my head anytime soon
What's worse is that you definitely don't feel the same way.
It hurts but soon enough I'll be over this and I'll be fine. I'll finally stop thinking about you.

Forever,
Jojo

Mix Tape Vol. 2 Letter To Rendezvous 81

Date: 11th April 2020

Dear Rendezvous,

Well it's clear that you're still trailing my mind
Time and time again I try to actually amputate you
But then again I tell myself I know my feelings
And I'll try to accept it but that just multiplies them
Because everything I do I think about you
Can you unhand me from this grip you have me in?
I've chosen not to be there but you seem not to let go without even knowing
Why won't you let me go?
I'm unable to so you have to help me

Sometimes I close my eyes in hope that I won't see you but you're there when my eyes are closed just as much as they are when they are open
I want to bore you the details about my day and kiss your nose just for the love of it
I want to play with your hair because my fingers seem fascinated with the feeling of it between them
I want to stare in your dark eyes and see that there is more that meets the eye
As they glisten in all times of the day and night
Just as they sparkle more when you smile

I want to hug you when I'm down knowing I'll feel better without you speaking
I want to inhale your perfume as it lingers after you're gone and only hope that you're back soon so I can smell it again
I want to feel your touch and the electricity it brings
I want to hear your voice and feel it's effect to my toes and the warmth it brings to my heart
I want to feel the heat of you next to me and how much my heart beats faster.

Now that I sit and write I see
When I create you're my muse
The only thing that I can't have that is constantly on my mind.

Forever,
Jojo

Date: 19th April 2020

There we were
Holding hands under the night skies
Where the stars twinkled
And they could bear witness that we were here together
Intoxicated in a way only us could understand
Safe, happy, secure, peaceful
And as we lay under the night skies in the sand
And the soothing sound of the waves I turn around and look right at you

But you are not here
You seem far, distant
And then I look clearly
But you are not here anymore
You were never here

Now I'm laying on the shores..
Sadness seeping through my pores
And the tide takes me and I let them as they engulf me with it's current

I'm underneath now
Cursing myself wishing I never saw you like that
Thinking about you in all those special places
But now I'm sinking in the deep end
Drowning slowly in the waters
But I'm not struggling
I let the water take me down
Falling deeper and deeper with this hole in my heart.

#AhiEgbodo

Mix Tape Vol. 2 Letter To Rendezvous 83

Date: 1st May 2020

My my, the mighty darkness
As it comes upon me in the night time
And I look up and there you are
In my head you shine bright
In the darkness you appear
And I will think of you till the end of time
And I will hum that song that I fall asleep to
And awaken for the night cometh to me again
I'll wait for the darkness and night skies and I'll think of you again and again
Until the sound of silence cometh upon me
And my words limited with my thoughts running wild
And shear goosebumps appear with just thoughts of you
And the night time becomes peaceful as I await for the day you can hold just then will my slumber recon with me.

#AhiEgbodo

Date: 18th November 2020

Dear Rendezvous,

I'm dumber than I think sometimes
You may never see this
I'm sad that I think about you so much and I still did this to myself
Allowed fear once again get me to do what I don't want to do
I guess I was using sex to hide how I really feel
I can't say that wasn't part of it but it wasn't the reason
I'm scared that I may never match or never be enough
I'm scared that you would get bored of me
I'm scared that I love you more than you love me because I do love you
I've let you you go now and I can never have you back
I'm going to have to live with that for the rest of my life
I'm to have to live with the fact that I let fear blind me
I'm going to have to live with the fact that I let you go. my slumber recon with me.

Forever,

Jojo

84 TEEN ANGST

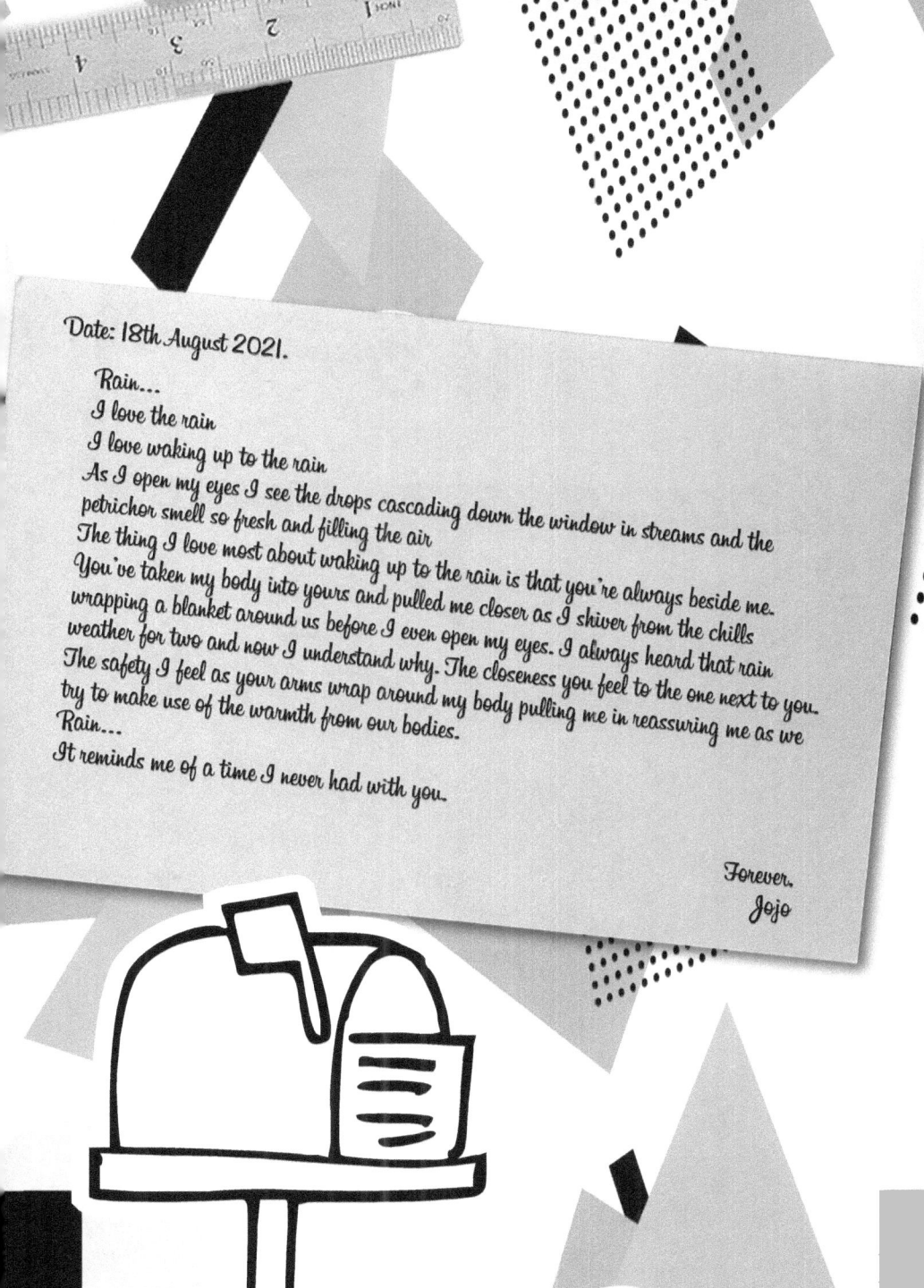

Date: 18th August 2021.

Rain...
I love the rain
I love waking up to the rain
As I open my eyes I see the drops cascading down the window in streams and the petrichor smell so fresh and filling the air
The thing I love most about waking up to the rain is that you're always beside me. You've taken my body into yours and pulled me closer as I shiver from the chills wrapping a blanket around us before I even open my eyes. I always heard that rain weather for two and now I understand why. The closeness you feel to the one next to you. The safety I feel as your arms wrap around my body pulling me in reassuring me as we try to make use of the warmth from our bodies.
Rain...
It reminds me of a time I never had with you.

Forever,
Jojo

Mix Tape Vol. 2 Letter To Rendezvous 85

TIMES LOST

Date: 2020

Who you were then: 19 about to turn 20. I thought it was the end of my life and I had to do something about it. *The old me*

Who you are now: I'm just 21. **Studying** masters in literature. *The NEW me!*

Times lost

So many things to do
Books to read
Unturned pages
Notebooks with Blank sheets
The trailers all seem great
My mouth can't stay shut this way
So many movies to tick off my list
With game shows and sitcoms
Time would you calm down
Take a breath and have a nap
I've been chasing after you.
Ever since the sixth grade
We gotta hit that new mall
It's uptown and the traffics wrong.
We need to try some new cuisine
But oh well another breakfast bar!
Time can you chill
While we take our notes atleast
Youth is slipping but you're dancing
Can you stop for a Lil while please?

I LOVE LARA

Date: 11/26/2020

The old me

Who you were then: grieving. For a second year in a row. I have not experienced loss like that before. It was profound, there is no better word to describe it. One of my dogs has died that day. I was always relatively sheltered from death in my life, but I am the kind of person that cries at funerals of near strangers. It feels extremely *privileged* to mourn a dog like that, but our pets are essentially my siblings – except for the fact they have a lot more hair. Lara had the most wonderful fur – **soft, and thick, and warm**, and so comforting. And never again could I run my fingers through it. She would never play with me again. She would never clumsily run my way to greet me. She would never lick my face again. For the first time in my life, I felt so empty, so broken, and so DEVASTATED. So I channeled those feelings into a poem. All the sadness and grief flowed through my fingers onto the keyboard. And here it is.

Who you are now: I think most of that sadness has stayed with me. And I suspect it will always be here. I am an adult now. I have to do **WHATEVER** adults are supposed to do, because I live and study abroad. I cannot mope around all day. All of this happened only a year and a half ago, but I had to change quite a lot. I still think about her, yes, but much less. I cannot fall apart every other day, that much I know. So I live. I still write quite a bit of poetry, but I mostly busy myself with the *mundane*.

The NEW me!

Mix Tape Vol. 2 I love Lara 89

Miss you

I Love Lara

I can still feel the soft weight of your body on my lap,

As if you'd faded away, right here in my arms.

I don't know what to think: where did you go?

Through the roof —

or into the soil that once gave birth to us all?

Where are you?

I miss you so much, what shall I do?

A thousand years have passed in my mind;

You left me alone to ponder in the dark.

As I stand alone,

With a void for a soul,

Great pining overcomes me.

I could never set you free.

I was born broken to the core

Always wishing for more —

Than just a simple life.

And I was once happy: when you were mine.

I held you so tightly an eternity ago,

You appeared beside me: like a god as a dove.

Oh, tender, sweet, beloved creature, come —

Right into my arms, I will take you home.

HOW DOES IT FEEL TO BE KNOWN

Date: 2020

Who you were then: A happy person. I was a person that was ready to things and get them done. A person who makes people proud especially my family. I had many friends as I had a positive attitude everyday. I was so *innocent* and *bright*.

The old me

Who you are now: A boring person. I have made myself a disappointment to people especially my family. I have a negative attitude every day and it has changed everyday. I have very few friends now and do not really talk that much. I have **failed** as the older I get but I am trying.

The NEW me!

How does it feel to be known? The same question is being asked in my head everyday. How does it feel for everyone to look at you? Talk about you? Hang out with you? How does it feel to have fame?

While I'm here alone, sitting or standing no one would notice me. I look in the mirror and realize, I am truly a nobody.

Like a fallen leaf from a tree, I am left behind on the ground. While everyone else is still on the branches, no one bothers to look down.

Sometimes I wonder, how is it possible to be recognized? I look around and see everyone but then I realize,

People are with people. They talk a lot with each other
and it's a beautiful sight just to see everyone together.

In the middle of the public I can feel the energy,
experiencing loud noises from people who are either mad, sad, or happy.

I ask myself again, How does it feel to be known? How does it feel to be popular? Be social? Be able to be seen?
After tiring my mind from thinking too much I finally know what it means.

It means to believe you are known, believe you are looked.
It means the people around you will finally be hooked.

Believe their eyes are stuck on you and not on them
Therefore, I'll end up with many friends.

Many friends means less time with myself
Am I happy now? Happier than I ever felt?

I finally know what it means to be known
It is not the paradise as expected.

I wonder if I'm better off alone
Although there is no decision I have regretted.

SOME PEOPLE

Date: 2021

The old me — Who you were then: My life was in a darker place and my reality just came crashing down on me.

Who you are now: I am healthier and safer and so much better and I am ready to share my story with the world. **The NEW me!**

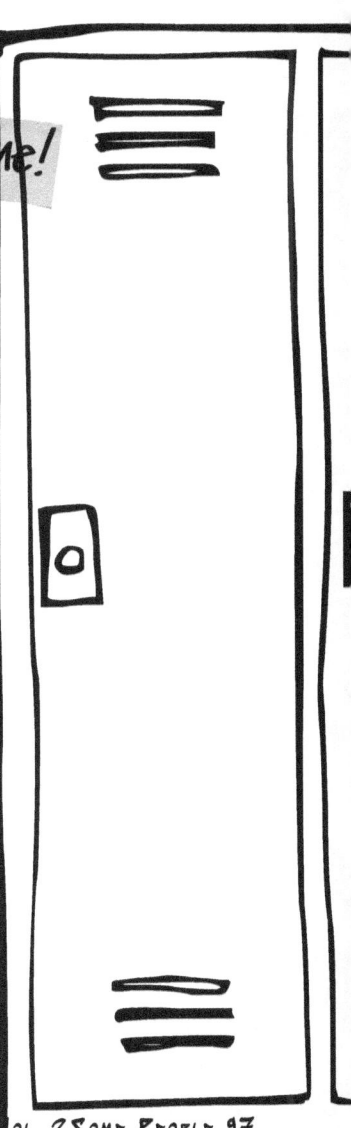

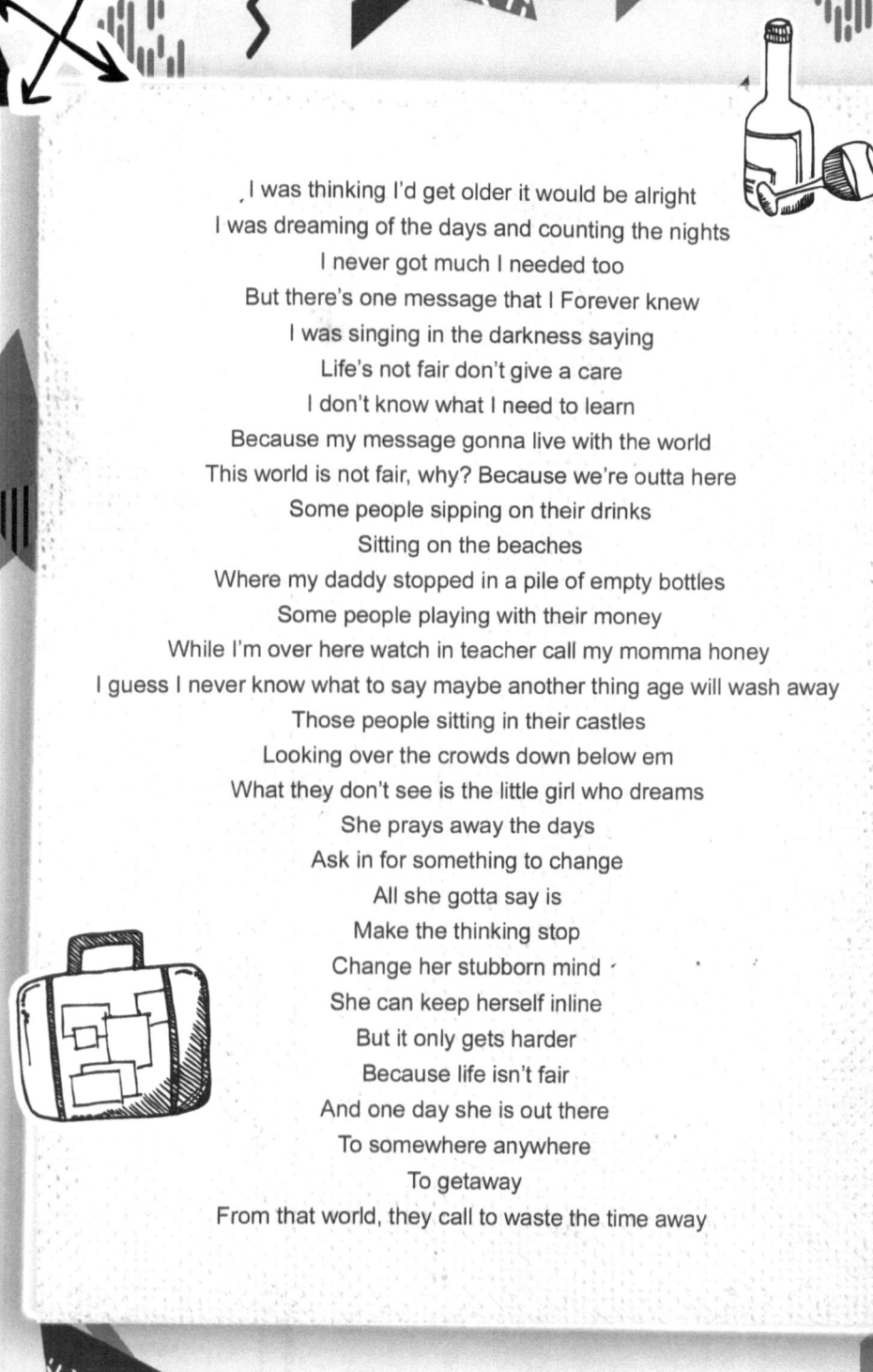

I was thinking I'd get older it would be alright
I was dreaming of the days and counting the nights
I never got much I needed too
But there's one message that I Forever knew
I was singing in the darkness saying
Life's not fair don't give a care
I don't know what I need to learn
Because my message gonna live with the world
This world is not fair, why? Because we're outta here
Some people sipping on their drinks
Sitting on the beaches
Where my daddy stopped in a pile of empty bottles
Some people playing with their money
While I'm over here watch in teacher call my momma honey
I guess I never know what to say maybe another thing age will wash away
Those people sitting in their castles
Looking over the crowds down below em
What they don't see is the little girl who dreams
She prays away the days
Ask in for something to change
All she gotta say is
Make the thinking stop
Change her stubborn mind
She can keep herself inline
But it only gets harder
Because life isn't fair
And one day she is out there
To somewhere anywhere
To getaway
From that world, they call to waste the time away

JAMIE

Date: 2021

Who you were then: During this time, Covid-19 lockdown just ended. And this was when I met a new friend and how things didn't really turn out the best.

Who you are now: After meeting this person I am doing better. I am a happier person without them.

The old me

The NEW me!

Mix Tape Vol. 2 Jamie 101

Jayden M
Creative Writing
Mrs. S
February 22, 2022

Jamie

So, this was about almost one year ago. It was spring break, and I was in Florida with my best friend Rachel. I usually go with her family every year. On spring break every year her dad's friends always end up in the same location as us for spring break. One of the families in particular had a son that was childhood best friends with Rachel. His name was Luke. I've met luke before so when I found out he was going to be in Florida with us I had no problems. Once we arrived, Rachel and I noticed that Luke didn't come alone. He had brought two friends, Leo and Jamie. Of course I knew who Leo was because Leo has been friends with Luke for over a year. Jamie on the other hand, I had no clue who she was. Supposably Jamie had just moved to our school, so she was new. Luke introduced us and she honestly seemed really nice. Throughout our whole trip we had a blast. Surprisingly Rachel and Jamie and I got along really well. On our last day of vacation we woke up super really to watch the sunrise. "Wake up" I said to rachel. "Ugh, It's too early for this. What time is it anyways?" Said Rachel. "It's 5am, now come on let's go Jamie's outside waiting on us." I replied. Rachel got up and we all eventually made it down the beach. The beach was only down the street, so it was a short walk. "Wow, it's gorgeous," Said Jamie. After the sunrise we all got breakfast and then went to the beach for the day. Later the night before we all left Jamie said "Hey guys, we should definitely hang out once we're in Fort Wayne." I said "Yeah! That sounds great".

The next morning it was time to leave. We woke up at 4am to pack up the car, just so we could be out the door by 5. The car ride felt short. We got home around 5pm, well 5:30pm for me because we arrived at Rachel's then she took me home. I was tired so as soon as I got home I fell asleep. I woke up the next morning to my phone blowing up. It's Jamie. She is already trying to make plans. The next thing you know were in a group chat, with only me and Rachel and Jamie. We ended up making plans for next weekend. As Friday approached we all agreed on going to Luke's house. Rachel headed over to my house and picked me up. Once we got to Luke's we realized Jamie was already there. "Hey guys, OMG i've you guys so much how are you?" said jamie. "We've been good," I replied. The afternoon went okay, Rachel and I started to realize Jamie wasn't a really good influence. She always joked about doing the most random things, and how she would manipulate her parents in order to get what she wanted. It was about 7pm when our other best friend Catherine texted Rachel and I to hangout. So we invited her to Luke's house. Things got pretty interesting once Catherine and Jamie met. "Omg! You're so pretty." said Jamie, "Haha thank you so much Jamie." said Catherine. Jamie was nice but seemed a little off from when me and Rachel met her. "Hey guys, I'll be back. I'm going to use the restroom," said Catherine. Once she left Jamie went off on how she hated Catherine for the way she was. "Guys how are you friends with her, she's paranoid all the time and super annoying," said Jamie. I go, "She's not annoying at all, she's really nice". We all were silent, Catherine slowly walked in. None of us looked at each other, we just looked at our phones. I ended up texting Catherine about the whole situation and she decided to confront Jamie to her face, right there in then. Of course Jamie denied everything, so we all just went home. I mean me and Rachel were both there to witness everything.

The next morning we woke up to bad news. Jamie died, or so we thought. All of Jamie's accounts on social media had posted that she had passed away. This couldn't be, so we called her father. "Hello? Who is this? ``said Jamie's dad. "Hi, this is Catherine I was just calling to see if Jamie is okay?" said Catherine, "Oh yes, she's doing great, she's just upstairs in her room." said her dad. I can not believe Jamie faked her death. So we all texted her. Blocked. After that day we ended up never really hearing about what happened to Jamie. Apparently she blocked Luke too and moved away. She taught me something that I honestly never want to go through again and that's introducing new people around people you truly don't even know. She also taught me when you first meet someone don't automatically think they're a good person just because of their personality.

LONELY

Date: 3/14/21

The old me

Who you were then: I was 16. We had just moved to a new town, and because I was home alone all day and didn't know anyone my age I was *extremely lonely.*

Who you are now: Now I'm 17, I go to a new school and I know a lot of amazing people. I'm in way more activities than I was when I was at my last school such as choir and track and *show choir.*

The NEW me!

> lonely
>
> Lost and alone,
> Or blaming myself again.
> No human can ease this pain.
> Embarrassed when speaking,
> Lacking when quiet.
> You don't understand that I am going insane.

Am I So Worthless

Date: 2021

The old me — Who you were then: A person who was a bestie of peace, with a mind who was in control

The NEW me! — Who you are now: Now I am a person whose mind is *crazy* as a dog on drugs and about peace and me and PEACE had some tussle and now we hate each others faces

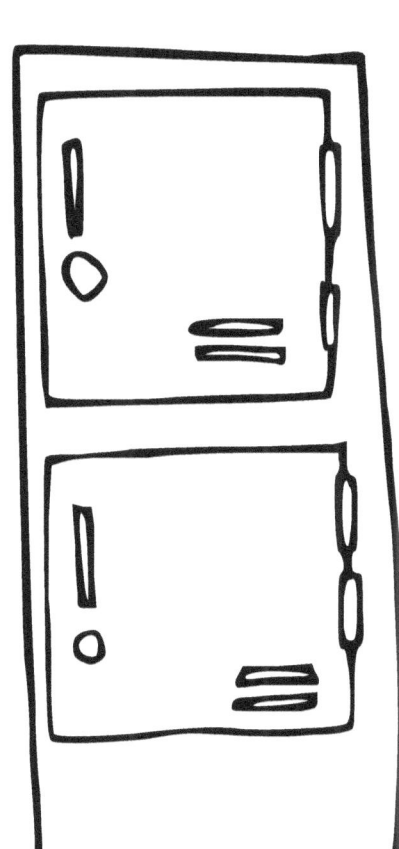

Mix Tape Vol. 2 Am I So Worthless 107

Am I So Worthless

Maybe benovent is not my soul
But what I try is whole
Maybe I give up a thousand times
But would that be considered in crimes
Am I so worthless
That you all have to give me a mirthless

Half population knows how to throw out tears
But who knows how to hold their bears .
Half of them know how to insult
But how many know how to consult
Maybe I am a shame
Never I am fitting in that frame
Am I so worthless
That you all have to give me a mirthless

They will never understand me
They will never try to understand me
Why will they care about my mind
Why will they care about my mind
Never will they become intertwined
But have they taught me to try your best to be strong
And never be ride along
Am I so worthless
That u have to give a mirthless

ESCAPE

Why is it always me who wheezes in sadness
Why is it always me made fun of
Why is it me alway who cries in the dark
Why do u alway leave me with the never going mark
I can remember all the bullying and emotional damage u give me
Maybe With the experience I can get a Low everything degree
Maybe I do a thousand mistakes
Maybe I do achieve a thousand failures
But Why do u always succeed in making my self esteem lower
Because u never and never try to know her
I am the glass
With a very weak point
I have a low pride
With a shame of mine
Am I so worthless
That's you have to give me a mirthless

By: A
Written in 2021

A person who was a bestie of peace, with a mind who was in control

Now I am a person whose mind is crazy as a dog on drugs and about peace and me and peace had some tussle and now we hate each others faces

UNTITLED

The old me

Date: 2021

Who you were then: I was just a *girl*, and I am still a girl. What happened, is that I never had a close relationship with my **father**, and now he's with me and I don't really get along with him, so I am trying to apologize

The NEW me!

Who you are now: I had a great relationship with my **father** now, but eventually we would fight...

Sometimes, I really don't like you
We were never so close, it's true
I just can't keep myself from hurting you
Because I felt like you hurt me too much to not giving it back
It seems like it's okay for you to lose me
So I pretend the same to not making myself break down onto the ground
I don't know if you love me, or really just you don't know how to describe
I don't know if you need me, it feels like without me everything will be just fine I love you but scared to see you around
It's been crazy and I'm sorry
But I guess we're a family, are we?

UNTITLED

Date: 2022

The old me

Who you were then: I was me, I wrote it a few months ago, going back to what had happened. My parents never get along, and they FIGHT, and it would be me who pick up all the pieces that left behind. I **cry**, and I want them to stop and apologize but they never does. It's like no one understand me and what I'm going through.

The NEW me!

Who you are now: I feel better now, and am still *healing* :)

She had a loving family
But she hurts because she lost it all
She has the pick up all the broken pieces
Trying to bring the love back in places
Hiding her pain with anger
Behind that strong face was sadness
She felt alone even there is someone besides
Because she knew no one ever understand what she's going through The memories were killing her softly
The screaming was hurting her badly
She has been loved
And now, she can hide
Where she will feel safe and sound

UNTITLED

Date: 2021

Who you were then: Back when I was in primary school, I had a BEST FRIEND who really never cared about my feeling, and I kept tolerate her for a long time, and never notice I forgot to love myself and put all the attention on her instead of me. She bossed me around and she talk to me WHENEVER she wants and never cared about me, it hurts a lot. I literally cried myself to sleep those days but still being friend with her, then one day, I **exploded** and fall out with her, it felt great, but it's like everything you spend on her was nothing worth.

The old me

Who you are now: I am trying to LOVE MYSELF first and doing the best to care for myself. And now I know even if someone is your friend, you can't let them just cross your limit.

The NEW me!

I always cried over people who don't deserve me
I called them my bestie, but all they do is ignore me
I forgot to love myself so I could love them
Never notice I lost my freedom
When I need them the most
Want someone to cry on
They were not around anymore,
They found someone better and left me alone
I spend days, months in the corner of my room
Trying to figure what I did wrong
Hurting, crying for someone who doesn't deserve my tears

UNTITLED

Date: 2021

The old me

Who you were then: Back when I was younger, I didn't do well in class and it's hard for me to concentrate. I felt so DISAPPOINTED in myself. I didn't tell anyone because I don't want other to think I worth nothing. It was scary, feeling I was nothing but unworthy and ungrateful to my parents. It hurts

The NEW me!

Who you are now: It's great, I CHANGED a lot and overcome everything and it's a brand new me!

I feel like I worth nothing
I tried to be good
But it all lead to the edge
I fell down the cliff
Every time when I tried to climb up
I fell again, it's tough enough to be back
I'm not worth anything
I want wings to fly
But always fall down the pale blue sky
I tried to cover my scars,
It's hard to hide but I will rise

UNTITLED

Date: 2021

Who you were then: My life was stressful at the time dealing with *college admissions* and school starting up again. I had also started my first job and I was dealing with adjusting to that as well.

The old me

The NEW me!

Who you are now: My life is not as **STRESSFUL** now since I less stressors. Right now I am getting ready for college and completing high school.

```
When I wake up
You are the first thing on my mind
I can't even begin to describe
How my heart races when youre next to me
When we met
You felt a rush of ecstasy
When my eyes laid an innocent look on you
I felt it in my veins
Love ran down
When I wake up
I realize what i'm feeling is not just a dream
What I am feeling is actually happening to me
Your presence brings me a thought
That can only be described as
'Till the end it's me and him"
```

3 YEARS

Date: 2021

Who you were then: I had just reached my 3 year *milestone* of being self-harm free. Shortly after this entry, I was ironically hospitalized for suicidal ideation. While my headspace was far from clear, I had *perspective* enough to be proud of such an achievement.

The old me

The NEW me!

Who you are now: I'm still a teenager, still full of angst. I'm coming up on 4 YEARS CLEAN from self harm this August, but this piece in particular helped me memorialize my struggles with mental health in a way I have never been able to articulate myself. FINDING priority in the memories of struggle has been an important milestone to my ongoing recovery.

Ozzy P
08-23-21

3 Years

Beloved is an overstatement, love being vacant, and "to be" unknowing. On my grave they will not know what to write, placing tribute to a name that has vanished and succumbed to self pity. I am not sorry for leaving you. I am sorry you never felt known by me. I never understood you as I sought to be understood desperately by those who would listen. I'll sacrifice my heart to the sky and maybe the clouds of disinterest will shed a new light of right. May the drops fall heavy and low, imposing on every thought you had of me; if any. How can I expect the fulfillment of minds in my presence if I only contribute to the decay of a rotting subconscious? I have myself to thank, for who else is self absorbed enough to dry swallow their pills and leave dirty dishes in the sink. As the garbage juice runs down my forearms, allow me to enjoy the warmth of a new day and the collapse of life. I want to pierce the thoughts of a new mind and greedily bite the hand that feeds me such thoughts; soon to be revealed as my own. And may that day come evermore.

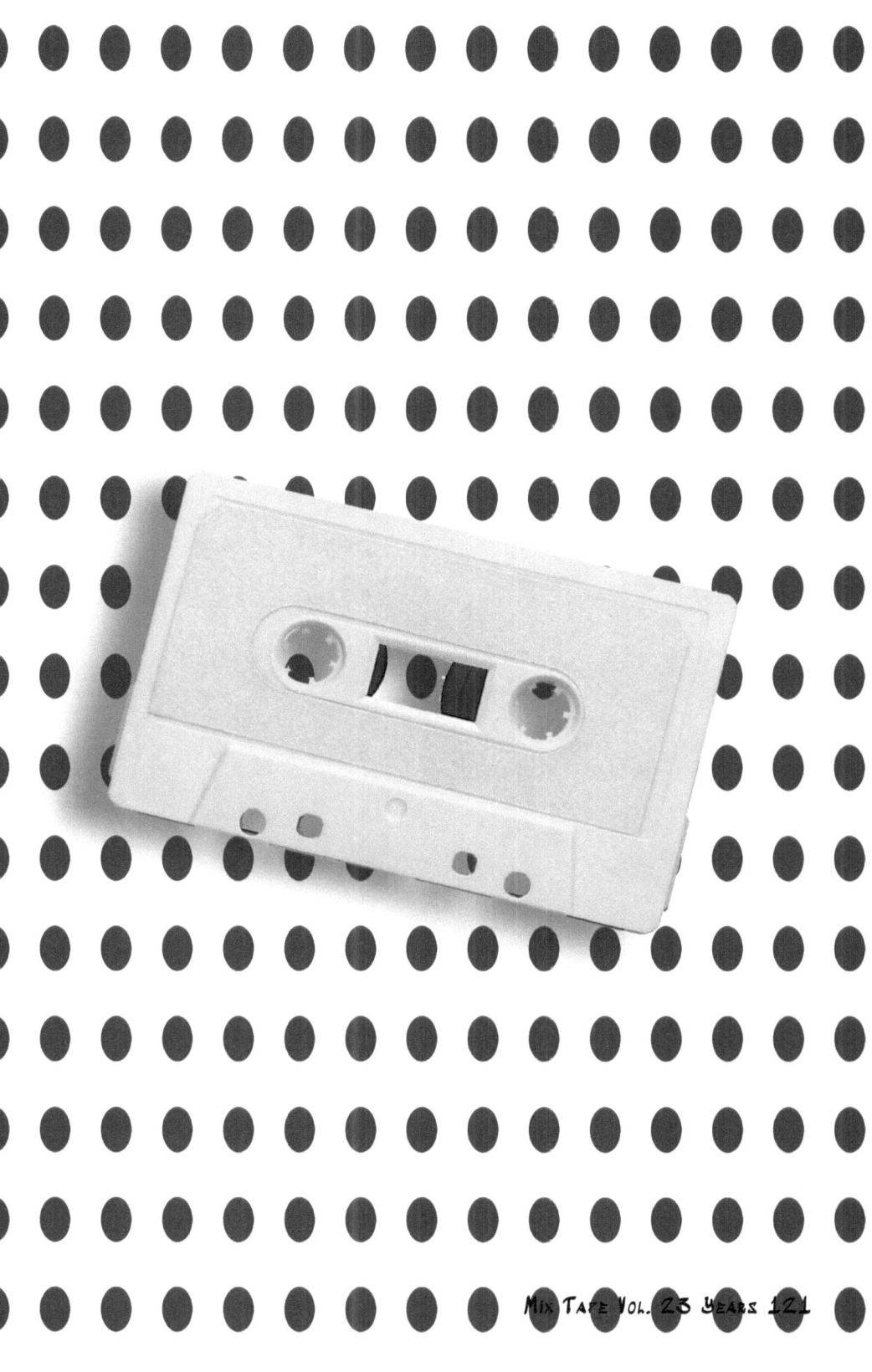

THE LAST GAME

Date: March 10, 2022

The old me

Who you were then: During the time that I wrote this *ballad* I had started to get close to a guy in one of my classes. We got close because of the class and up until this week we were just friends. His friend and my friend were dating and we sat with them, which forced us to sit together. Our paths crossed at so many points throughout the years but for some reason we never really paid attention to each other. He liked to pick on me, mostly making jokes about my height. The fact that he could make me **LAUGH** and comfortable about my height at the same time, made my heart warm. For the next few weeks every time I walked into class my cheeks would turn bright red and my stomach would fill with *butterflies*. I know it sounds crazy but he was my inspiration.

The NEW me!

Who you are now: I would like to give you hope, telling you that it worked out between us and we got our *happy ending*. Yet, I would be giving you false hope. Things are not the same between us for many reasons. I learned a lot from my time with him. I am content with my relationship status, enjoying my time with friends and family. Truth is, I don't know if I am ready for a relationship. I am learning how to be on my own and I'm *thriving*. You also don't never know what the future holds. Now I am focusing on me. My school work, sports, and my health. Its refreshing. I will always be *grateful* to him for helping me write with creative poem.

The Last Game

He loved the game more than many things
When it was his last one
A bitter taste filled his mouth
This... was his last run

He loved the game more than many things
The adrenaline rush and cheering crowds
His teammates who by his side
Nothing but net when the buzzer sounds

He loved the game more than many things
The way the ball felt in his hands
The joy of a win and the pain of a loss
His loved ones cheering for him in the stands

He loved the game more than many things
But not as much as he loved her

She was his better half
One he did not want to live without
She was the one for him
This truth he had no doubt

When he woke up
Before he went to bed
She was the one he thought of
Always on repeat in his head

She was the light to his darkness
The fuel to his flame
The support she gave him
She was his everything

When the final buzzer brought the last game to an end
He celebrated with his team
But the whole time he was looking for someone
She stood in the crowd looking like a dream

Making his way towards her
She wrapped her small arms around his neck
In that moment he was happy and content
She reached on her tippy toes and gave him a small peck

Her presence was the only thing he needed
She knew who he was inside and out
Her love was all he needed
He was in love with her without a doubt

Date: 5/27

The old me
Who you were then: I was very lost in life, and realizing how much my **father** impacted my life

Who you are now: I am still lost but knowing that my **fathers** wsidom will stick with me gives me *hope*

The NEW me!

Do you know of someone that you couldn't imagine your life without? Because I do. My dad has inspired me, motivated me and shaped me into who I am today. My dad is is the strongest man I know in my life. He whom has shaped me into the person I am today, has taught me countless lessons that I have valued every single day of my life. There is not a single person that could have made even half the impact on my life, as my dad. He truly is my greatest hero. He has picked me up during some of the utmost hardest times of my life.

My dad is my biggest inspiration in life. Ever since I was a young girl, he has taught me something anywhere we go. It doesnt matter if we were just out eating, he still had something to teach me. I am not exaggerating when I say I could name 100 quotes that have stuck with me from him. Wether its sports, school, life he has advice for it all. He has taught me that even the most successful people in life have all failed. You have to fail many times before you succeed at something. My father has been here every step of the way. I have gone through something I hope nobody else has to go through in their life, but to be brutally honest I would not be half the person I am today without it. My dad has shown me that there is a light at the end of every tunnel, to never give up and to persevere through this journey we call life. As my dad says, life is a marathon, it is not a race. He has taught me it is okay to be different than everyone.

My father has motivated me in ways nobody else ever has. When my parents recently went through a divorce, it impacted me a lot and took a huge toll on my life. My dad, who had just lost his mother, was in a very bad spot in his life. How many kids can say they've seen their dad cry before? I don't think a lot can, but I can. It was probally one of the most heartbreaking things I have ever seen. It made me realize how he has always been there for me, and he's always busy worrying about us kids, and Ive never seen him go through something personal like that. Of course it affected me that I had lost my grandmother, but even more that my dad was going through so much. I knew it was my time to pick my dad up and try and understand what he must be going through. These past couple of years I have really realized I owe him the world. He has pushed me so hard in life but has raised such a grateful and strong daughter because of it. Our family has been through so much, to say the very least. Honestly, I wish things could have gone much differently, but at the same time I am blessed to have gone through it all. I am just so much stronger because of it all. I have such a different outlook on life than I ever did before.

My dad has shaped me into the person I am today. Words will never be able to describe how blessed I am to have a dad like mine. Not everybody can say that, which makes me so grateful every single day that I do. I would be so utterly lost in life, especially at this moment if it were not for my dad. He is one of the richest men I know. And no, I am not talking about money. I am talking about knowledge, about how pure his intentions are for his kids and his love for his family.

My father has inspired me, motivated me and shaped me into who I am today. I have been through so much, but above all that, it was a learning experience. It made me know exactly what I do want and what I do not want out of life. It made me a lot stronger, a lot more independent and it made me have a different perspective on a lot of things. My dad is my greatest inspiration, and forever will be. No man will ever have a greater impact on my life, I am tearing up even writing this. Reminiscing about all the memories I have of my dad showing me what life truly is about. Not about the fame, money or fortune should ever matter if you have love. He has shown me what its like to truly care for people, he is one of the most down to earth people I know. I will always look up to my dad, and I will always be his little girl. I hope to make you proud dad.

And I Smile

Date: March, 2022

The old me

Who you were then: I was having a **BREAKTHROUGH** and a real hard time. Noone was there to help me and everyone was repeating the same generalised, idealised thoughts. I was finally able to recover but not in the generalised way people have defined those thoughts to me. It was totally different and I was in a oasis of *serenity*.

The NEW me!

Who you are now: I'm still having a rough time but I'm **STRONGER**. I like this version of myself better.

Mix Tape Vol. 2 And I Smile 131

I hate myself.
I spare no effort in befriending people,
But I am vague and unexpressive.
The slightest change hurts me.
Everyday is an emotional battle for me,
I hate everything here.

Until something happens,
Something happens that hit me hard.
To the core of my heart it pierces,
And i realise how hard i've been trying to keep stitching my heart and soul.
And my eyelids half shut,
I feel myself fatigued and worn out,
And i smile.
But this smile ain't any pretend,
Ain't very wide,
Just a slight smile it is,
That comes from within.
I accept everything,
Not considering it good or wrong.
And that is when I know,
I embrace my tragic life
I embrace my anguished heart
My weary and jaded head
I'm carefree of what people have imposed,
"To smile bright" go all beaming out.
I kept trying so far and it knackered me down.
I find my comfort in the "disapproved" smile.

I dont need light.
I dont like the bright.
Something again what fellows have told me to stay in.
I kept stepping forward,
Even though it kept kicking me back

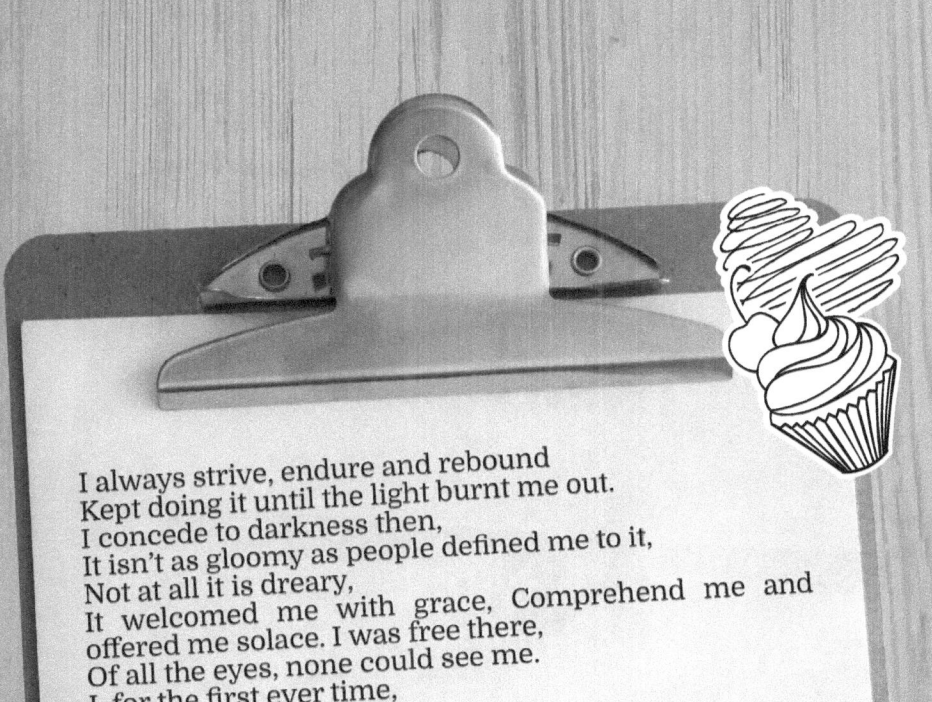

I always strive, endure and rebound
Kept doing it until the light burnt me out.
I concede to darkness then,
It isn't as gloomy as people defined me to it,
Not at all it is dreary,
It welcomed me with grace, Comprehend me and offered me solace. I was free there,
Of all the eyes, none could see me.
I, for the first ever time,
Could utterly be myself,
And not be in delusion of "being myself".

At once I knew this is where I belong,
This is where I could breathe in ease.
It limits my vision but also expands it,
It frees me of trivial things
that isn't worth of bothering me,
And unties me from the fears of being debacled and lonely.
I love me.
I love the company of my own.
I befriend people who are attracted to my personality.
I can transcend my emotions.
My feathers are not ruffled by anything.
I am free of all humanly battles.
Everything is a delight to me.

1-22-22

✗ Date: 2020

The old me — Who you were then: I was 15 and I had just gotten *broken up* with a guy I thought was going to be with me FOREVER.

Who you are now: Today I'm still going ◯ stages of getting over him. *Life* has more friends that have been with me thr◯ I've been going out more and socializing.

The NEW me!

MIX TAPE VOL. 21-22-22 135

1-22-22

If I had my phone right now, I could distract myself from the crushing truth by scrolling through social media and never thinking about it again. As of right now, I'm alone in my head, knowing he's never coming back. The truth? That's the bigger question. Did he ever love me? Did he just use me for his own happiness? Not knowing the truth is like getting a **BRAND-NEW CAR** only to find out there's no engine.

You try your best to fix it. Take it to a mechanic, try searching for the part on GOOGLE, but searching for the right answers never comes up. It's only false truths and the pain of your head spinning. Around and around like a merry-go-round. Those are fun, with the bright beautiful colors and the children laughing, the colorful horses going up in down. My merry-go-round has no laughing children, it has no colorful horse, it's just *endless spinning.*

Rack your brain all day and night, then you think, let's take the brand-new car back to the source. They'll have the right answers. The source? They're gone. Never to talk to you again. Is that how it works "these days" When he breaks up with you with no explanation, they're never supposed to be seen talking to you? Maybe there is no truth. Maybe this is God's way of telling you, that you don't want to know the unbearable truth. I've heard many versions of the truth, but these can't be true... right? Not unless it comes from the source. Here we are again. The source. It's a constant loop. Should I talk to him? Yes. Definitely...maybe not. Maybe he's already giving out brand new cars. Maybe the engine works on these cars. Was I different? No? Maybe being different isn't always a good thing.

Being a kid that loved this car with everything couldn't possibly see the bumpy road ahead. Too busy looking at the marvelous brand-new interior and getting distracted by the brand-new car smell.

What if I would have taken one more deep breath in. I would have realized that that brand new car smell was mold slowly growing getting stronger and stronger as time went on. Look around this brand-new car he gave you was used, it's dirty. If I would have just looked again. I would have seen this car for what it was.

I'm just a kid on a **merry-go-round**. How could I have known? They say "you'll find another car; it'll be way better than this one" but what if I wanted this fake car. What if I miss the ugly smell of it, because all that mattered was that I had this car. It was all I needed. Well, what's a car without an engine? Hope? You think well the source will come back and he'll give me a brand-new engine. Is that one going to be used to? Would it matter? If I had an engine, I could drive it, right?

Let's just go back in time to when I never had this car. No. This car brought me happiness when I felt like nothing else could, but it was all a lie. What are you not getting? Maybe kids shouldn't have cars. They get too attached to the idea of it all. Is the truth that I was the one that didn't know how to work the car? Is it my fault? I love this car; it couldn't be my fault. How would I have known; the source is gone. "Your chat is pending." "Not delivered try again." "The person you are trying to reach is no longer available."

Why do I want to know the truth? Let it go. I can't. Did I spend four months looking for an engine that never existed? My car was **ONE OF KIND** he said. Why is he giving my car to everyone else?

I always wore a seat belt, but why put on a seat belt with no engine? For the pain sticking truth. Maybe deep down I knew that the car was fake, crashing at any moment. Was the seat belt fake? Was I stupid enough to trust everything he said? When I was in this car, I was safe from anything. Without an engine or a seat belt, how could I be? How could a car move without the two? The short answer is I pushed. I pushed this car up and down a steep, 1000 ft tall hill if I needed to. Whatever it took for him to love me back. Maybe I saw the crash coming, I let it happen. Why didn't I stop it?

Maybe you needed more attention than what I could give you. I just wish it wasn't from other girls. You tell me "It's just hard for me to open up to people." then why does it seem like everyone knows everything about you but me. Somehow you always needed my attention. If not mine it was another girl's attention. You lied constantly. The attention. That's what you craved right? Wanted me to feel sorry for you. When I questioned what you were saying, you turn it around on me like you do everything. You say I'm selfish and self-absorbed. "Why don't you believe me?" "You always think about yourself. How up self-absorbed can you be?!" aren't you the one self-absorbed? Always said I should take your side and always worry about you 24/7.

Romeo and Juliet. They used to be my role models, two people that fell in love, two people that would do anything for each other. Maybe I thought I was in a fairy tale to even think that I was all he wanted. Was I in a *fairy tale*? Just for a moment. Maybe your hearts were beating at the same time. For just one moment it felt...real. Now that it's over I can see clearly.

What is it people say? Right person wrong time? Maybe you were the right person right time. I wish I could say I never loved you as you did me, but that isn't the truth. I took our picture off the wall and the love letters you gave me and ripped them up. Was that enough to forget you? Forget the person I thought you were? I look at the photos when I was with you, I was truly happy. You made me feel something I've never felt before. I loved you so much that even when he didn't respond to my messages for hours, broke up with me with no explanation, and left me **heartbroken**, I still tried to understand him. Understand how some I was willing to spend my whole life with was able to do something like this. You say you hate me. You say, "just move on. Get on with your life, I fell out of love with you a long ass time ago.".

Is it easier to hate me than love me? I want to know the truth. It's all I've ever wanted to know from the beginning.

"I think its best if we part ways...*goodbye*." Those words felt like hitting the bottom of a never-ending hole. Was I relieved? I could finally breathe without the chore of worrying about you. Dating you is having a different problem every day, I didn't care because I wanted every piece of you, even the worst parts. Now instead of a different problem, it's the same problem every day. You broke up with me in front of 100s of people. My chest tightened. My pulse raced. My hands started shaking. I was out of air.

If I had an option to do it all over again I would. As badly as it hurt in the end, I would give anything to feel the happiness I felt when I was with you. Do you remember the beach? We were in the water together; my friends were all partying onshore. The sunset painted the sky with bright blues and deep oranges, purples, and soft yellow colors. You said, "the *sunset* is almost as beautiful as you." As the deep dark blue water surrounded us, you held me close. I splashed water in your face, we laughed until our eyes met again. Your beautiful baby blue eyes consumed me. We grew closer. That was our first kiss. Just us. Together. You weren't thinking about any other girls then. It was just us, chest to chest, sharing the same air. Time stood still at that moment. I wasn't worried about anything else.

I took off my seatbelt willing to crash. With you and only you. I couldn't get enough of you. I was addicted from the first time I met you. You were my drug. What's an addict without their drug? All that's left is a craving, a craving for more. I knew that you were hurting me, but I thought if I kept fighting for us it'll be all worth it in the end. Was it worth it? There's no longer an "us" it's just a painful memory, a broken record.

Maybe there was never an us, maybe it was just a foolish girl fighting for a boy's attention stupidly thinking that her fighting wouldn't just push him further away. Your friends now know me as the egocentric girl that never cared about you. Maybe loving me is the reason you can't love yourself. A *ghost town* is all that's left. Everything we built together is gone as if it was never there in the first place. Streets that were once filled with love are faded away. Isn't this what he wanted? "He *loves* me, he *loves* me not." Even as a little girl on the playground picking off petals from a daisy, I wanted to know the truth. In some ways my flower is dying faster than I can pick the pedals, never knowing the truth.

When you give your all to someone you lose yourself in the process. Social media tells us that you should always put yourself first in your relationship. What if the only way not to lose him was to put Him first in every situation even if you were drowning in the deep end. Was it enough? Where did it all go wrong? Maybe putting you first is what you thought I should have done. Doing that took control of the person I thought I was. My days became **SURROUNDED** by you, and I was okay with it because I had you. Now that you're gone all I'm surrounded by is silence. It's as if I'm in space. I can't tell if this stillness of it all is sickening or peaceful.

I still catch myself worrying about you. If you're okay. If you're doing things you're not supposed to be. My friends say, "you're not my **PROBLEM** anymore", but what if I want you to be my problem. Yes, hating you is way easier than loving you, but how can I be doing both? Do I just hate you for the way it ended? How easy it was for you to just cut me off and move on. I would've walked through hell and back for you. Maybe you're just as broken as I am. Trying to put back all the pieces that once were something. It's the hardest part; piecing together a puzzle in the dark not knowing where the pieces go. Maybe one day I'll find my new **HAPPINESS**, even if it's not with you. I wanted everything to be you.

People said that I changed you in the best way possible. They say that they're so happy for us, but why did you let them tear us apart? You did things that I would have never done to you.

So why am I so stuck on you? You said you would never leave me, but then your bags were packed. Was I too much to handle? Maybe that's what I get for opening up to someone.

That's something people never tell you about the one you thought you once loved. How they can just get up and leave you whenever they want. The unstableness of it all. Even the constant reassurance isn't enough. It's never enough. You risk it all being with someone you truly love. The risk is terrifying but EXHILARATING. Being a pretty girl in a world with other girls that are better than you in every way is having that thought always in the back of your mind. "I'm easily replaceable to him" Feeling replaceable is having a pit in your stomach. Every time you look into his pretty blue eyes you fall deeper and deeper in love, but the pit just gets larger and larger. Maybe it's the "gut feeling" he's going to leave you. Personally, it was me warning myself "you're too attached" I was lost in him. None of it mattered. He was mine and I was his.

We crashed. The old you didn't make it out alive. Our road is a dead end now. Maybe it's for the best. You showed me the real you and I'm sad it took this long for me to realize it. One day I'll stop tearing up when I think about us, my **heart** won't stop when you walk into a room. One day, I'll be okay without you by my side. As of today, I must face the truth. My truth.

ALWAYS THE MAN

Date: 5-11-22

Who you were then: Before I wrote this I was in a relationship that I thought was a healthy relationship and I was **IN LOVE** with a person

The old me

The NEW me!

Who you are now: I am out of a relationship and it's the same routine but I've been working on myself, I'm working on my mental health, my physical health and my emotional health but I needed to write this to get this off my head

This dormant heart
Is turning cold
Staying away from the warmth
That you use to give
But this warmth you left
Is starting to ignite

All things I did for you
All the love I gave
The speech you always made
That you were a real man
But in the end withered
The meaning of love

As always
I'm resigned to be the man
Never receiving the flowers
I'm getting exhausted
From this constant routine
When will this end

Random First Line

Date: 2022

Who you were then: I was still me. **STRONG** emotions and mania + a break up make for a very good piece of writing.

The old me

The NEW me! Who you are now: So many **places**. Mostly bad.

Just when she thought she'd finished crying, the phone rang. She knew it couldn't be him, he had no desire to call her anymore. Her sister ran to answer the phone. As her sister picked it up, she wiped her eyes and attempted to stop her hands from shaking. It turned out the phone call was for her mother. She let out a sigh of relief, followed by a sigh of disappointment. She decided she would go outside, get some fresh air, and clear her head. On a night like it was, the sky should have been full of stars, but as she looked up, her legs almost gave out. Would she ever love again? He had been her healing, and now she would fall back into the darkest places. Three times now, she'd almost died, and no one had noticed.

She wished she could go back to that night, back to the hospital. She began to remember the phone call she'd had with her real mother that night. Her voice broke over the phone as she said, "It's actually pretty nice here." She had tried to make her mom feel better. To make sure she didn't think it was her fault her daughter had wanted to die. Later that night, when the dark thoughts came to haunt her mind, her body shriveled into a weird shape on the uncomfortably crooked hospital bed. She had never known that a human body could twist into that position. As she lay in that awkward place, she thought about her home life. Everything about her was a lie.

She made a poor job of hiding the damage she had done to her own thighs and wrists. Some nurses looked at her with empathetic looks, some with questions in their eyes. As she came back from that memory, she thought about the events that happened that same night. She thought about all he had said, and remembered how her heart stopped as she read the texts, one heartbreaking line after another. He wasn't cruel about it at first. But by the time he was done, she was in hysterics. For the last two months, they'd been inseparable. Her life and mind were often unstable things. With him

though, she'd had some wonderfully stable times. With sadness, she'd realized they needed some time apart.

He needed time to live his best life, and she needed time to heal. She knew he'd start to see the world in more colors than ever before, while her life became colorless and dreary without him. Too many thoughts corrupted her head. So she did the only thing she thought would help. She ran. She sprinted down the street until her feet ached and her calves threatened to cramp. As she stopped to catch her breath, she looked back behind her. For a second or two, she could have sworn she saw him. His tall, slender figure standing in the shadow of the street light. His dark blue eyes pierced hers. But when she blinked, he was gone. She could have sworn it was him, couldhave sworn he was there. She silently sobbed into the cold sky and fell to her knees. Her mind was playing tricks on her now, and she couldn't stand it. She became furious. How could he just ask and expect her to move on so easily? How could he ask her to forget all the magical moments and memories they shared, to leave their love behind? How could he betray her so easily?

The questions never stopped coming, while the answers for them never arrived at all. When she got home, she ran to her room to find the one memory she knew she could keep of him. As she searched her bed for the stuffed animal, her movements became frantic. Her eyes threatened with tears and her mind raced a mile a minute. She had to find it, to hold it. She wanted to hold it and treat it with the love she always wished someone would give her. The love he gave her.

That night, her mind flooded with dreams and stories of him. Mostly memories, but also vivid clips of the future they could have had. As the dreams faded from one to the next, she chased to grasp at them, forlorn. A couple days later, she was still in despair. One last time, she asked him for one last call. All she needed was to hear his voice one more time. As she sobbed on the other line, whispering "sorry" in between gasps, he said it was okay. She had never heard him sound so cold. As he muted his line, she crumbled onto the floor. With more apologies stuck in her throat, she hung up. She couldn't take it anymore. She wept and cried uncontrollably until her body fell limp.

She wanted to be cold. To be heartless. But she often found she was only broken and wretched, proving she had more of a heart than she could bear. Her cave had collapsed. She kept breathing, but she was no longer living. She kept her head up for as long as she could. And now, she's crumbling. But she's also learning and healing. I'm she.

UNTITLED

Date: April 11 2022

Who you were then: Well it was last night, actually, and I was feeling especially **ANGSTY** about the girl I like and how we can't be together because we live in a homophobic community.

The old me

The NEW me!

Who you are now: Pretty much the same, since I wrote it yesterday

if i were to kiss you
id kiss you with the weight of a thousand feathers
if i were to kiss you
id kiss you in the hidden corners
of this all seeing prison
if i were to kiss you
id kiss you with my eyes closed
and my mind full of hope
yet i know i'll never kiss you
not here
not now
not yet
i can't kiss you
because our love is taboo
and we're trapped
trapped together yet far apart
but, if i were to kiss you
id kiss you with the hope of acceptance
if i were to kiss you
i would kiss you to the sound of dreams
if i were to kiss you
id hope you'd kiss back
id hope you'd leave your fear behind
and if i were to kiss you
i would kiss you with a silent promise
a promise to help you
a promise to save you
but alas
it's only a dream
a dream i always wake from
because i cannot kiss you
but maybe if i were to kiss you
then i would not wake up
and we would be free
no longer trapped
in this all seeing prison
oh, if i were to kiss you

Untitled

Date: April 23, 2022

Who you were then: Upset at the world and felt jaded and annoyed at the scrolling on social media, the explotation of workers, and the failure to feel as if I have a future at all. It felt as if my ideas for the future can only stay as ideas not because i can't do it but because I am unable to do it due to the situation of our current world.

The old me

Who you are now: It was only a few days ago so I feel similar but I want to hold out hope that my dreams will not stay as dreams

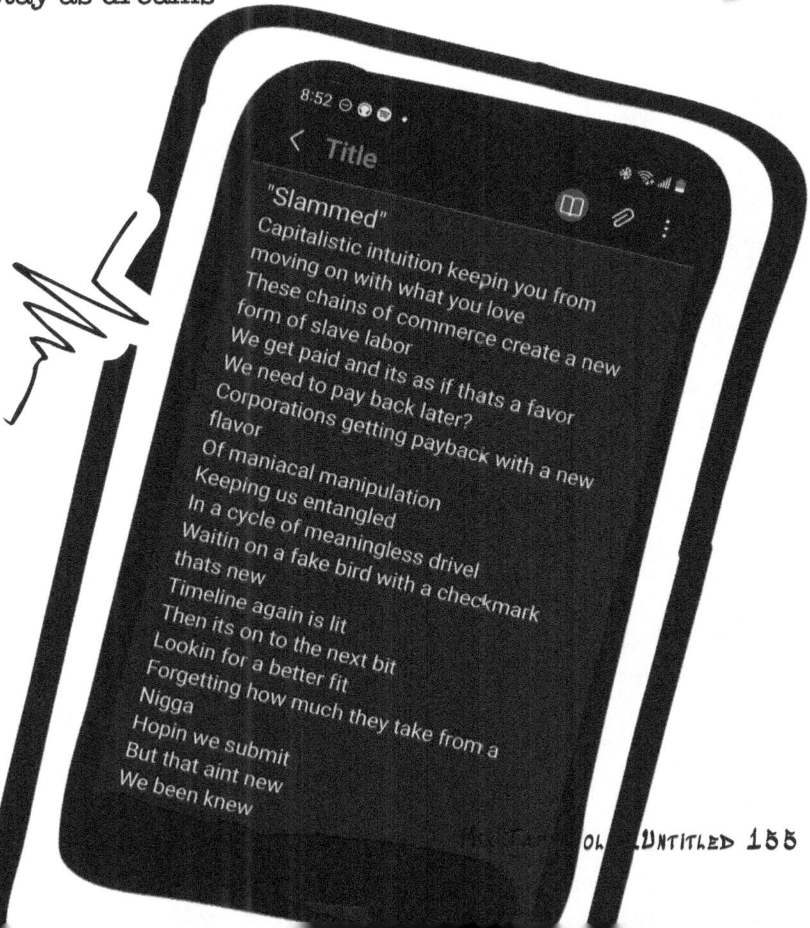

The NEW me!

"Slammed"

Capitalistic intuition keepin you from moving on with what you love
These chains of commerce create a new form of slave labor
We get paid and its as if thats a favor
We need to pay back later?
Corporations getting payback with a new flavor
Of maniacal manipulation
Keeping us entangled
In a cycle of meaningless drivel
Waitin on a fake bird with a checkmark thats new
Timeline again is lit
Then its on to the next bit
Lookin for a better fit
Forgetting how much they take from a Nigga
Hopin we submit
But that aint new
We been knew

The many give so much to the few
Then they ask us to kneel behind the pew
Wait for your offering
Here Nigga chew
Still smilin sayin bless
Shootin achoo
Got us all puppy eyed we aint gotta clue
Even when they chokin us blue
We still fightin over hue
Tillman get shot in the head, man who?
Flag on the play but the jets still flew
Questions arise its all just for fuel?
They say the foul is up for review
But who checkin they crew
Who knows who behind the man who
behind the man who behind the coup
Waitin in the wings for your cue
Cant even speak when all your facts are true
Silenced like when Chuu sue
Choked up hanging from the noose
Wringing the adams apple for some juice
God thats some strange fruit
12 lurking forgetting they can choose
Reppin the 99 look its Terry Crews
While 911 protecting the Howard Hughes
Flyin around with no excuse

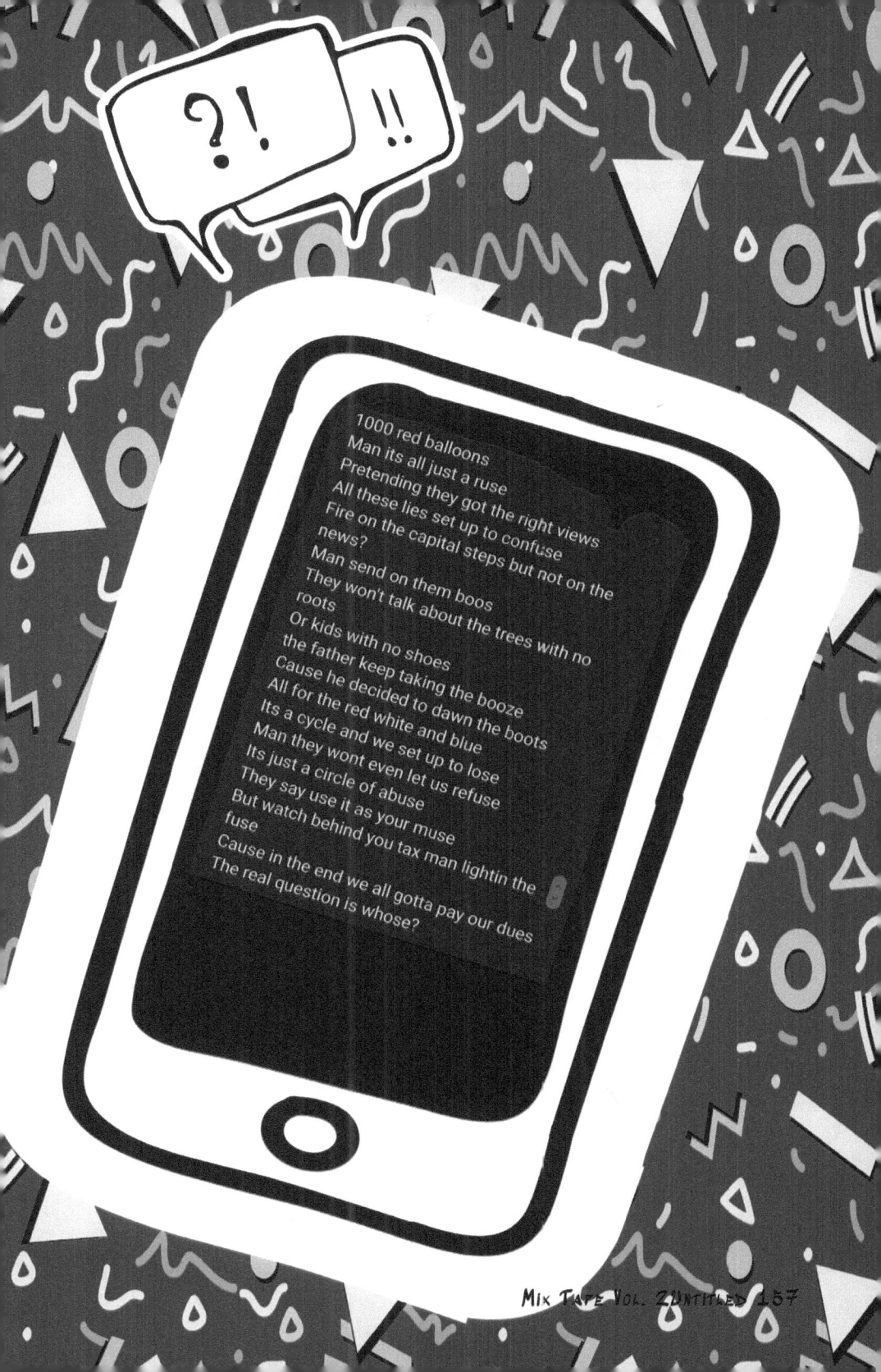

I BELIEVE IN NOTHING

Date: November 2021

Who you were then: At the time this was written I was not in a **good relationship**. I was all mixed up with life, struggling with four mental disorders, piled on with suicidal thoughts, cutting, stress, and more. I was a Freshman in *HIGH SCHOOL* that was getting told by people to kill myself. I was sexually assulted twice, lost a lot of close friends, and had a lot of people not liking me. I was at my lowest, and I had written this prompt. The theme was "*I beleive in...*" It was nothing. Nobody showed me what love was really like. This relationship I was in lasted for a long, toxic year, and I didn't even know it. I poured my **HEART** and SOUL into it, and it's something I look back at and try to remember how I am growing and adapting from it.

The old me

Who you are now: Now I *beleive* in love. I had people pick me up, yes, bring me down too, and overall teach me lessons. Shortly after I wrote this story, I met this one guy. He taught me how I should focus on myself and know when to take a step back and give time to myself. I loved him more than anything, but when he told me he still liked me but he wanted to be just friends, I held my ground, wanting to still have this loveable, cuddly 'boyfriend'. We never put the title on it, but it was better than any other relationship I've ever been in. When I stayed put, standing up for myself, I started to get petty without even realizing. He ended things, **blocking** me on social media, but not iMessages. I gave him his space, greiving

The NEW me!

over it all. My goal is to try to get him to at the least understand my side. I never told him I loved him. That's where I am now, though. Still struggling with depression, anxiety, ADHD, anger issues, suicidal thoughts, my addiction to cutting my skin, and more, but I am over the ex-boyfriend. I find that as a big accomplishment, and I'm sorta proud of myself for it. I am still LEARNING, *growing*, and developing, but I always have my down moments. If I had to tell readers one message, it would be to remember the reason you've held on for so long. Scars may cut deep, but it's your decision to either make it even deeper, or HEAL and **grow** from it and have it as a reminder to keep pushing through and looking at the light at the end of the tunnel.

Paige Dilluvio
November 2021

I Believe in Nothing

It was a Monday, on a bright sunny day. I drove to his house, not allowed inside because we were home alone. We dug up a basketball from a dusty bin and started playing a version of horse. He and I played this, but instead with the word, "us". The only thing that mattered to me in the world, and the only thing I believed in. <u>I *used* to believe in *us*.</u> We used U-S instead of H-O-R-S-E because we were one another's favorite things, but mainly being that we both were horrible when it came to basketball. Neither of us could score if our lives depended on it. As we were laughing and building our love for one another, it suddenly started to pour. I, not being too fond of my clothes getting soaked, dashed for the garage. As I'm at the speed of light, I feel a tug on my wrist. The hand tugs me towards it, pulling me closer, as he presses his lips against mine. Our feet begin to waltz about the concrete, as the cold drops of water flash before our eyes. We could do nothing but gaze into each other. Our hearts were overflowing with passionate love.

His parents had arrived home, so we walk inside, dripping wet. As we slip off our soggy shoes and socks, we let a soft smile glance at one another. We then pull on our matching pajamas and snuggle in the basement with warm, fuzzy cats in our laps for the rest of the night.

It's now Tuesday. We had busy work in the morning and evening, so we agreed to call at dawn. We each open our laptops, revealing a big, white shein, shimmering on our faces. We then open a shared google document titled "The Future Of Us", as we start jotting a bucket list of cute dates we'd like to plan doing later on in our lives. I fall asleep, unnoticed, snuggling up with his stuffed Orange bear, and his sweatshirt. I wake up to him still being on the phone, admiring me.

My heart skips a beat, feeling cared for and adored. "I mattered to someone", I thought. Talking up a storm, the two of us seem to stumble up against a parasite of an argument. It was so unimportant to me, I couldn't tell you what it was even about. There is a rage firing out of him, lava bursting out the seams of his pale but soft skin. He has had enough.

Speeding over to my house for the first time in months, we both came to the side of my house, blank faces. Under his subtle breath, his voice shattering, he muffles, "I don't want to do this. I want to be with you, but I can't." My overflowing heart suddenly starts to pour out.

"W-what? What do you mean? I love you! You can't just-"

"I love you. So much."

"THEN WHY-" I'm interrupted again and again when all I was going to do was try to put back the pieces that he was pulling apart.

"Look, I'm sorry", he says, sobbing. I have never seen him cry this hard in the year we had been dating. He was a beautiful, happy sky, that shed a few raindrops here and there that suddenly had a thunderstorm. We cried in each other's arms, which somehow pulled me closer to him.

I wanted to be with him forever, as he did too. I know this because on Valentine's day, I walked downstairs into his basement, and he was wearing a tuxedo with a red bag in his hands, with a flowerpot, along with my favorite candies. Inside the bag was a Mickey Mouse snowglobe with a picture frame. He happened to buy two of these at Disney World when he was 6. His young self said, "I am going to give this other one to the person I want to spend the rest of my life with." Ten years later, it ends up in my hands. However, now all I had was a broken heart that was caused by the only person I felt loved me.

We both wrapped up our thoughts. I stated that this is not what is best for me, but if it was the best for him to break up, I'd do it if it would make him happier. He explained how it wasn't going to be good for him now, but it would be in the long run. We both departed, teary-eyed. The pain that was left behind was a knife that had been stabbed into my heart, and when it was taken out, there was a burning sensation left for me to deal with. **_I believed_** that **_he didn't love me anymore_**, and he proved that to me by not messaging, calling, texting, no nothing. How did we go from kissing and dancing in the rain on Monday, planning our future together on Tuesday, to the terrible Wednesday? For four months, I felt nothing but sorrow and hurt. The only person who had ever loved me left me, and that thought lingered beside me like a shadow that just won't leave you alone.

Summer is over, and we're getting into the 21/22 school year. Only three weeks in, and I get a Facetime call from him.

"I'm still in love with you." I was so confused, still being in love with him. My own feelings had conflicts. I believed that he didn't love me anymore, and I refused to change my mind on that until he would prove it to me. I don't know what to believe, so, **_I now_** believe in **_nothing_**.

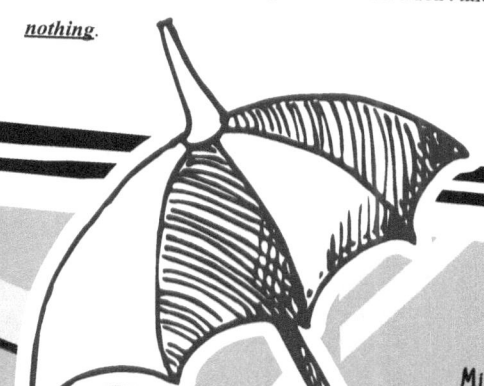

Poems 1,2 &3

Date: 2021/2022

Who you were then: back when i wrote those poems i was just getting my life back together after a long time of a *creative block* and **identity crisis** i was discovering my likes and playing around with different topics and trying to create something new again

The old me

e NEW me!

Who you are now: today i have found myself and my **identity**, i am now able to fully express my ideas, myself, my random thoughts through my writings

Poem 1:

Our love was created by Aphrodite and that's why our love wasn't the sweetest story. Our love was like Psyche's and Eros, for one is struck by cupids golden arrow. Our story was written by Aphrodite whose is eternal suffering just like Orpheus love for Eurydice. but I would fly as high as Icarus if it meant being with you, for I swear by the river Styx I will always love you. matches were more curses than blessings,

Poem 2:

Day or night? They always asked. But what about dusk and dawn? What about that time when the sun first shines waking the birds so they can sing and fly? What about that time when the sun says goodbye casting the world in a golden shine as the sky cries in a shower of beautiful colors? Day, night, dusk, dawn; I wouldn't choose one but all.

Poem 3:

is the bad guy really the bad guy? I ask myself sometimes. we are always seeing the world through the hero's eyes but what if we saw it through the villain's eyes for once. what would we see? a man so full of hunger for power, born evil ready to destroy the world? or would we see a man so broken by the world, a man that had to time to grieve and heal, a man who is in his own way trying to right the cruel world that the hero is so set to save, a man who is protecting himself from harm, a man who only wants the love that the hero recieves? And if we look deeply through the hero's eyes would we truly see someone born an angel with such a pure heart ready to die for the greater world? or would we see someone who thrives on pride, someone with a big ego, or maybe someone so confused thrust into this world his fate already sealed, does the hero truly truly believe in the greater good or is he just doing what he was asked to do? I have no answer but what I do know for sure is that not everything is what it seems to be.

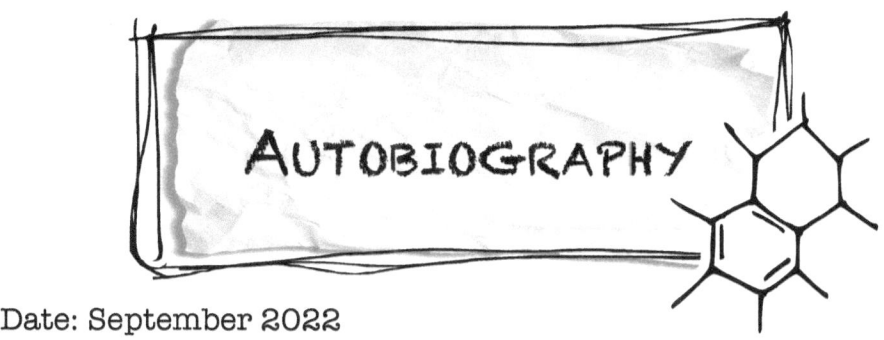

AUTOBIOGRAPHY

Date: September 2022

The old me — Who you were then: I was just starting school being hopeful after an awful year beforehand but ready for a *new start*.

Who you are now: I am more positive about the year now and I have a **new motto** for myself that is, "I'm gonna have a cool story one day".

Autobiography

Some of my most significant memories growing up are fairly pointless but they are the main ones to stick around in my earlier years. When I was 3 or 4 I remember eating a lot of pizza at my birthday gathering. Later on in elementary school in kindergarten we were all menaces. There wasn't much to do on the playground so as kids in 2009 we would pull up long weeds and use them as whips and slap each other with them all year. As the weeds grew more boring some kids decided to catch bees and hold them stinger out and chase you around with the bee. I never got stung and I suppose that is where my running career started. There was one kid I am kind of proud of for myself in kindergarten. He was a bully and he and his friend were chasing me and I was running in circles around a jungle gym for a few minutes then juked him out and he hit his head in the jungle gym and I got called to the principal's office. I could proudly say I didn't do anything to him. That was pretty much the highlight of my first few years of elementary school. As I move on to middle school I have a pretty quiet 6th grade year because I was very much so unfortunately misled. I was one of the kids to wear actual chakie shorts and bright polo shirts. My sister mislead me into wearing those items. For the next two years of middle school I ended up finding a pretty fun friend group and played baseball with some of them. This group all took robotics together and had a really fun time messing around with random things and we actually competed very well in competitions. Unfortunately that group followed each other to shreve and I made the baetter choice of going to Byrd. So then freshman year rolls around and once again my sister mislead into wearing the wrong things because I wore chacos to school once and I wore Nike socks with tennis shoes once and I got made of so I will never wear either of those items again to date. Freshman year I also played four sports which is not a very good idea at all. I played soccer and baseball and I also ran track and cross country. Soccer and cross country would never conflict scheduling but baseball and track did. I played baseball for byrd freshman year and had off campus there and I would never be able to get to track at a good time so I would run there in my baseball pants and gear and I must have looked very funny running laps around the track in full baseball gear. I really enjoyed baseball mostly because I got to hear so many stories and meet new people I would never have really talked to otherwise. I quit baseball after that season because it conflicted with track so much. I also ended up quitting soccer that year so I could completely focus on my sport being running. Sophomore year was pretty good up until February when it wasn't, I didn't have a main friend group but I was in all the friend groups. Then school got out for covid and it hasn't been the same sense. Last year was a huge struggle for me but this year is going to be good and I'm going to do well. That brings me to this summer. This summer I went to a younglife camp near the start of summer and got covid there, then the week before school started I went to New Smyrna Beach in Florida. This beach is the shark bite capital of the world and that's not a huge deal because i am not very bothered by sharks but this was one of the best trips of my life because for one it had been 4 or 5 years since our last vacation and the waves at this time on the beach were the biggest I had been inside in person. Each wave was consistently 15 feet out of the water and came in every few seconds. We also almost missed our flight on the way home because security had to open my mom's bag but I went ahead and got on our flight and my parents just barely squeezed in as they were closing the doors. Eventually after a lot of traveling hours i got back home the day before school. That catches us up to now and I am excited for this year and I know it can only come up compared to last year.

Date: 2022

Who you were then: was a *senior* in highschool and was working full time

Who you are now: going to college and meeting NEW PEOPLE

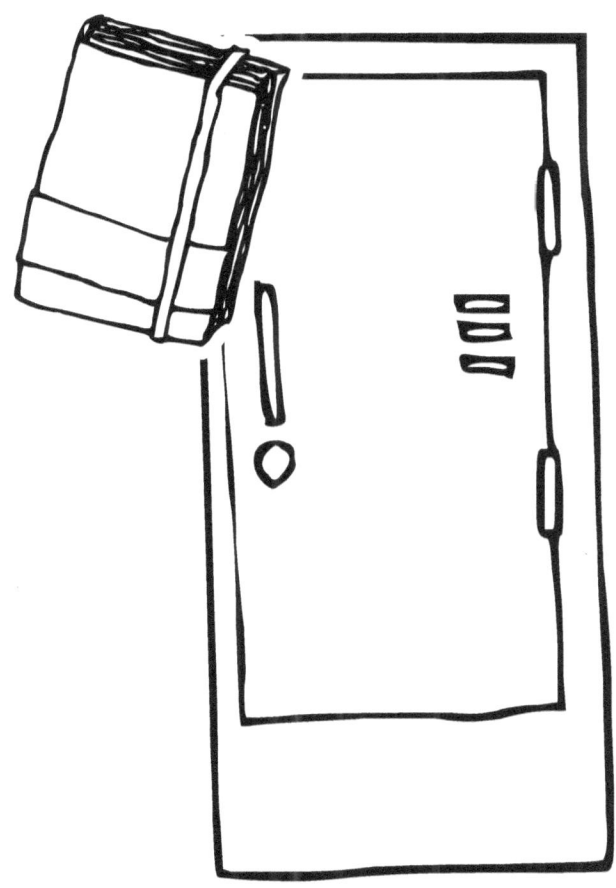

Kate F

Mrs. C

Creative writing

11 April 2022

Ella was just a normal girl, she enjoyed normal things, like music, and hanging out with her friends, but most of all, she enjoyed getting attention. She would do anything for attention, whether it be changing her looks, faking an injury, or even sometimes disappearing for a few days to see if anyone would check on her. Nobody thought it was out of the ordinary for her to be missing like this, sure maybe this time it was a little bit more extreme but definitely not surprising.

It was just 2 days before valentine's day that people heard about her disappearance, but it was also 2 days before Alex Miller's party. His party was supposed to be the biggest party of the year so of course, that was the only thing people were talking about. Either way, there was no way Ella would miss her boyfriend's party, she needed the attention. Her best friend, Morgan seemed to be the only one concerned, yes Ella had done stuff like this before but this time it was different. The night she was last seen, Morgan and Ella were hanging out, like every night, but Ella had said that she needed to talk to her brother about something so she had to leave after only being together for an hour. As for as Morgan had known Ella wasn't very close with her brother so she found it a little odd that she would ditch her for him. She didn't think much of it until Ella wouldn't answer the phone that night. Ella had lied about stuff like this before, just last week Morgan and she had planned on getting their nails done and Ella had said she couldn't because

her mom wanted to go shopping with her. Not even an hour later Morgan had seen her at the movies with her boyfriend but was too scared to say anything. So surely this was just another one of her stupid lies, morgan thought at first, but then when she didn't answer her phone and didn't show up to school the next day she started to get worried.

It was now the day before the party, still, nobody had heard from Ella, still, nobody cared. Morgan usually ate lunch with Ella, Alex, a couple of Alex's friends on the football team, and then whatever one of the player's girlfriend's names was. Today everyone was there, except Ella of course. Morgan thought one of them might have an idea of where she was, or trying to figure out something, but to her surprise, as soon as she brought up Ella's name everyone at the table started talking bad about her. Alex said he didn't care and had more important things to worry about and with him being the captain of the team, everyone else agreed with him. Morgan thought maybe since he was Ella's boyfriend she thought he would put at least a little bit of effort into finding her, but now it was confirmed that she was the only hope of solving this.

That night Morgan went home and tried to figure out what exactly happened the night Ella went missing. She had said she was going to talk to her brother so Morgan decided to text him. Sure enough, Ella had lied and her brother said he hadn't talked to her for at least a week. Since she had turned off her location on every app they shared, Morgan had no idea what to do next. She figured the only other thing she could do was text Alex to see if he was with her that night. When he did respond all he said was that she was being rude and acting weird that day, but by that time Morgan had already given up for the night.

It was now the day of the party, people had thought Ella would've returned by now, after all, when she had done this before it had only been 2 days. Now it has been 4 days without a

single word, post, or even text from her. People at school talked about it a little more today but nobody seemed to be too concerned, she still had a couple more hours to return before the party.

    People had started showing up to Alex's party around 6:00 p.m.. MOrgan was planning on going with Ella but had still not received a text from her. She didn't want to go to the party at all now that she knew this was a more serious case than people thought. With no leads on where she could be and nobody to talk to since everyone was at the party, MOrgan decided to go. She sat alone for the first part, talked to maybe a few people, but other than that the first part was pretty lame. After a couple hours ALex had gotten a complaint about the noise and had decided to ignore it. After failing to turn down the music, the police showed up. Nobody wanted to be caught so everybody ran out of the back and into the woods. MOrgan followed a couple of the football players that sat at her lunch table. She couldn't see much except a couple flashlights from other people in the woods and all she could hear was the loud music from the party behind her. MOrgan had thought her night was over until she heard somebody a couple of yards away on her right screamed. SHe went running to them, a group of about 4 girls were standing around what appeared to be remains of something. By now the police had caught up to them but seemed to be more concerned with what they were looking at rather than the fact that they were at the party. The police had told the girls and Morgan to go home and that they would deal with what the girls had just found.

    The day after the party was a saturday so Margan was planning on sleeping in late, however, around 8:00 a.m., HEr mom had woken her up and told her that Ella was on the news. MOrgan got up in a rush and went to the living room where her family was watching TV. She had thought this might be good news and maybe they had a lead on where Ella might be, or maybe they had even found her. However, MOrgan was not about to get the news she was

176 Teen Angst

expecting. She had sat down on the couch when the commercials ended and when the broadcasters had started to talk she knew this was not good news. As it had turned out the remains that she and the group of girls had found the night before, was the body of Ella. Morgan had no idea what to do, say, or even think. "Why would somebody do this to her?" "Who would do this to her?" "WHy did it have to be my best friend?" All of these questions were racing through her mind. The next day was Ella's funeral. She thought it was weird being there because she had this mindset that everyone she knew was invincible and not a single person would ever die. Especially Ella, never ella. As Morgan left the funeral she thought to herself is this it? Someone just dies and life goes on and they just live a memory in our heads. Of course Ella was different, no one knows how she died or for that matter who killed her. It will forever live with all of us. Especially because the killer was still out there.

Peace

Date: 2022

Who you were then: Umm...I was still 14 and exploring my poetry skills, just trying weave beautiful words together to have them like warm sweaters comforting in the winters. I was heartbroken, sad, anticipating, grateful, betrayed, trying, trying and so many things all together. I'd released like three songs on SoundCloud and yearning for a record deal.

Who you are now: Well...I'm still 14 and all of the things that I was back then when I wrote this.

Peace

Gloomy gales caressed my face
Like the bitter sea kisses its shore
And all my deeds died with grace
As I lay rotting like before

My eidolons crooned too sweet a tune
To the scarlet firmament above
Swiftly my July skipped to June
As flew so high the black dove

And then my voice found its home
As I let my heartbeat cease
And like the end of every poem
I blew like breeze and this was peace.

Dusk of the night

Beauty there is in the dusk of the night
More than there is in any praised sight
I could loiter around under this ocean
Of the depthless navy draped over my heaven

Charm there is in the touch
Of the frosty wind that is my much
Adored gift by the splendor of the night
That I ardently dream of during my respite

I could forever amble my way down here
In this lonely alley deemed rather drear
But how could someone not commend the way
The dusk of the night leads my wicked astray.

The Moon

There's this orb which when inside I cry
Gives me this grin that makes me not want to die
That shines not-so-bright, yet guides me enough
In the dusk of its background; when the path is rather tough
For every star has a dark background
But its remains obstructed without a sound

Like a parent lulls their baby to sleep
And a sibling quotes life, in a manner too deep
It camouflages me from my long abhorred nemeses
And makes me feel worthy, often with emphasis
Then I feel caressed, by its distantly gifted shelter
Oh how I feel so cherished; while indeed not in the center

Its spirit beckons to me; with that uplifting smile
As it gazes back at me, being farther apart than a mile
And no bed of coziness; has ever comforted me more
Than its dazzling diligence, which makes me try every door
Then swiftly it drowns back, to a heaven fairly unknown
My heart surely bleeds; but I recall how it shone.

Dear Moon

Gaze down at me every time I look up
Smile back at me when my eyes spill out syrup
Always guide me when I'm lost in the dusk
Spare some home for me when the rest world goes brusque

Have your craters always adorn you
Like jewels commend a nearlywed's value
Come in different shapes; I'll croon the same tune
May it be crescent, half, or full moon

Oh and tell the twinkling orbs surrounding you
That I indeed, adore them too
And forever remain the pearl of your ocean
For when this land becomes hell, I shall seek your heaven.

July

Around the end, of the month of July
Was a bijou born, with a billion attempts to try
She shone just dazzling, while no one really noticed
Her smirk was self-effacing, forever since remotest

The jewel had few plights, about which she was sure
And she endured all of them, staying still pure
Pouring glow, not wincing at scars, finding no cure
Flaring at the felon deceits, who were making it sore

The bijou had this view of life
That the whole plot was but a strife
That eventually she'd rest on the death bed
Ergo she never deemed worth the things her admirer said

Those two scarred beads
Belonging to the one who admired our bijou's deeds
June, who looked up to the gem of July
And July who never knew why the beads wanted to pry

June had a sight
Quite vague; but all the same saw light
She strived, for those dreams somewhat blurry
But for July she had a shoulder, even though in hurry

And as long as a mess persists, July ought to know
That June would be there, surely cry to cut sorrow
And July must not be, scared to lose a heart
For June would be there till the end, albeit not from the start.

www.ingramcontent.com/pod-product-compliance
Lightning Source LLC
Chambersburg PA
CBHW030231100526
44583CB00013BA/826